REAL FRAUDS FOUND IN GOVERNMENTS

BY LYNDA DENNIS, PH.D., CPA, CGFO

Notice to readers

Real Frauds Found in Governments is intended solely for use in continuing professional education and not as a reference. It does not represent an official position of the American Institute of Certified Public Accountants, and it is distributed with the understanding that the author and publisher are not rendering legal, accounting, or other professional services in the publication. This course is intended to be an overview of the topics discussed within, and the author has made every attempt to verify the completeness and accuracy of the information herein. However, neither the author nor publisher can guarantee the applicability of the information found herein. If legal advice or other expert assistance is required, the services of a competent professional should be sought.

> **You can qualify to earn free CPE through our pilot testing program.**
> **If interested, please visit https://aicpacompliance.polldaddy.com/s/pilot-testing-survey.**

ISBN 978-1-119-72331-8 (Paper)
ISBN 978-1-119-72335-6 (ePDF)
ISBN 978-1-119-72337-0 (ePub)
ISBN 978-1-119-72332-5 (oBook)

Course Code: **746562**
CL4RFGO GS-0419-0B
Revised: **February 2020**

V10018781_052820

Table of Contents

Chapter 1

Case 1: External Financial Reporting

Learning objectives

- Determine relevant fraud risks relating to management override in a fictitious government.

- Identify how management override of internal controls can lead to possible fraudulent financial reporting in a fictitious government.

Before we start

This case involves compliance with bond covenants on an interim and annual basis and reporting required information to rating agencies, trustees, and other oversight entities. Because noncompliance with bond covenants could have a material effect on a government's financial statements, it may be considered a significant risk area. Additionally, the potential for management to override existing controls to manipulate financial and operational information to be in compliance with bond covenants might lead the auditor to identify this as a fraud risk area.

Management override is an area of concern for auditors because management may be able to easily access data and systems. In addition, employees may be reluctant to discuss management abuses during the auditor's fraud inquiry procedures. Management override most often occurs in the following areas:

- Journal entries
- Estimates
- Business rationale for transactions
  - Bribes and kickbacks
  - Billing schemes

AU-C section 315, *Understanding the Entity and Its Environment and Assessing the Risks of Material Misstatement* (AICPA *Professional Standards*), states the auditor should obtain a sufficient understanding of the entity and its environment, including its internal control, to assess the risk of material misstatement of the financial statements whether due to error or fraud, and to design the nature, timing, and extent of further audit procedures. Fraud risk factors are events or conditions that

- indicate an incentive or pressure to perpetrate fraud,
- provide an opportunity to commit fraud, or
- indicate attitudes or rationalizations to justify a fraudulent action.

In all areas of the audit, the auditor is responsible for maintaining professional skepticism, which requires an ongoing questioning of whether the information and audit evidence obtained suggests a material misstatement due to fraud may exist. The characteristics of skepticism may help auditors better understand this concept of professional skepticism.

Characteristics of skepticism include the following:

- Questioning mind. Be disposed to inquiry with some sense of doubt.
- Suspension of judgment. Do not pass judgment until appropriate evidence is obtained.
- Search for knowledge. Investigate beyond the obvious with a desire to corroborate.
- Interpersonal understanding. Motivations and perceptions can lead to biased or misleading information (or both).
- Autonomy. Maintain self-direction, moral independence, and the conviction to decide for oneself.
- Self-esteem. Maintain self-confidence to resist persuasion and to challenge assumptions.

Knowledge check

1. Which is **not** an area in which management override may occur?

    a. Billing schemes.
    b. Journal entries.
    c. Estimates.
    d. Price fixing between two vendors.

Background

Jackson City[1] is a full service, medium-sized city in the west with a relatively small full-time population and a significantly greater population throughout the summer and winter seasons. In the last 40 years the city has grown significantly due to the increased popularity of its ski resorts and enhancement of area state and national parks. Although it is a medium-sized city, Jackson City is one of the larger cities in the state.

To continue to make the city attractive to the ski and hospitality industries, the city council approved issuance of utility revenue bonds to construct a $100m nuclear power plant. Due to the harsh winter storms impacting the city every year, increasing electric power reliability was of great concern to area residents and businesses. The plant was expected to increase the reliability of electric power to citizens as well as the ski resorts, hotels, restaurants, and entertainment venues. As part of the plan to finance the debt service and subsequent operation of the power plant, the city anticipated selling capacity in the plant to the county and other neighboring cities.

When the bonds were issued five years ago,[2] the county (through an interlocal agreement with the city) agreed to purchase up to 30% of the plant's capacity over the following 10 years. In addition, two neighboring cities were interested in purchasing capacity at some point in the future. Debt service requirements were structured to ensure no principal payments were required until one full year after construction of the plant, which occurred two years ago. Principal requirements in the first two years of operations were at reduced amounts and at level amounts for the remaining 28 years of the bond life. Interest incurred during construction was capitalized in accordance with the requirements of GASB Statement No. 62, *Codification of Accounting and Financial Reporting Guidance Contained in Pre-November 30, 1989 FASB and AICPA Pronouncements.* For the last three years, interest expense has been recognized.

Over the last five years, commercial growth in the city has been rapid while the growth in the permanent population has been slower than anticipated. Unfortunately, the county's population and economic growth over the last five years has not occurred at the level anticipated. To date, the county has purchased only 5% of the plant's capacity and it is uncertain when, or if, the county will purchase the remaining 25% of their committed capacity. Under the bond agreement, proceeds from sales of capacity

---

[1] All organization names used are purely fictitious as are the individuals depicted therein. Any similarity to real organizations or persons is purely coincidental.

[2] The Governmental Accounting Standards Board (GASB) issued Statement No. 89, *Accounting for Interest Cost Incurred before the End of a Construction Period*, in June 2018. Under the requirements of the statement, interest costs incurred during construction are expensed in the financial statements prepared using the economic resources measurement focus. This statement is applied prospectively and is effective for periods beginning after December 15, 2019. In this case, the power plant was constructed prior to the issuance of Statement No. 89 and the interest costs incurred during construction are properly capitalized as part of the cost of the related capital asset (under the requirements of GASB Statement No. 62, *Codification of Accounting and Financial Reporting Guidance Contained in Pre-November 30, 1989 FASB and AICPA Pronouncements*).

are required to be deposited into a debt service reserve fund and used to fund principal payments during the last 10 years the bonds are outstanding.

Knowledge check

2. Which is accurate of Jackson City?

    a. Jackson City is a full service, medium-sized city.
    b. The city has grown rapidly over the last 20 years.
    c. Jackson City is one of the smaller cities in the state.
    d. Jackson City issued bonds to construct a new water treatment facility.

The city and the trustee for the bonds entered into a number of covenants with respect to the utility revenue bonds. Should any of the covenants be violated, the bonds may be called by the trustee. Specific relevant covenants are illustrated in the following list:

Jackson City Utility Revenue Bond Covenants
Annual assessment (post-construction) of utility rates to ensure coverage of the required debt service ratio
Imposition of increased utility rates should the annual rate assessment indicate current rates will be insufficient to ensure coverage of the required debt service ratio
External rate analysis to be performed every five years (beginning in the fifth year of operations) by a qualified engineering or electric utility consulting firm
Maintenance of an average annual collection rate of 95 percent of commercial billings and 90 percent of residential billings
Maintenance of utility billing receivables aging at 80 percent due in 30 days, 10 percent due in 60 days, 5 percent due in 90 days, and 5 percent due in over 90 days
Annual actual debt service coverage ratio, based on amounts in the audited financial statements, of at least 1.15 throughout the term of the bonds
Adequate general liability and property insurance (including replacement value) covering plant and equipment
Proper maintenance of the plant and equipment
Conduct all inspections of the plant and equipment as required by relevant federal and state laws governing nuclear power plants.
Annual audited financial statements prepared using generally accepted accounting principles (GAAP)

Quarterly reporting, including quarter and year-to-date

- monthly billings by customer type;
- monthly collections by customer type;
- aging of receivables by 30, 60, 90, and over 90 days.
- certificate of insurance for the plant and equipment;
- certificates for inspections performed;
- internal and external rate analyses performed; and,
- amounts spent to maintain the plant and equipment.

For the first two years of operations, the city was able to project revenues adequate to cover operating costs and debt service requirements. Amounts due for required principal payments increase in the current year and the internal rate analysis indicated the city should raise rates an average of 10% to meet the required debt service ratio.

The case

The following exchange occurs between the city's finance director, Michael Lee, and the accounting manager, Brandon Scott.

"Brandon, when do you think you will have the electric utility rate analysis finished? We are coming up on the beginning of the budget process and I want to make sure we don't need to be talking about a rate increase. I'm not sure the Chamber of Commerce or the Economic Development Commission would be happy to hear we need to raise utility rates."

"Michael, I have good news and bad news for you. Which do you want first?"

"Let's have the good news first. It's Monday and I don't want the first thing I hear at the office today to be bad news."

"Well, the good news is I knew we were coming up on the budget cycle and I spent the better part of last week on the rate analysis. The bad news is, it looks like we need to raise rates about 10% across the board."

"Wait, I don't understand why we need to raise rates much less as much as 10%. What's causing the increase?"

"Remember the bond agreement allowed for lower principal payments the first two years the plant was operational but then increased them significantly in the third and following years? It's the increase in the principal requirements, making the rate increase necessary."

"I guess with everything else going on I forgot about the increased principal payments kicking in next year. Send me your files and I will go over what you've done to see if there is any tweaking we can do."

"When are you going to give the bad news to our esteemed city manager?"

"I don't think it's necessary to say anything to John at this point. Let me see what your numbers look like before we go crying 'fire' to him."

Michael looks over Brandon's rate analysis during the following week and finds it to be well done and reasonable. The following exchange between Michael and John Rogers, city manager, occurs a week after Michael has finished his review of the rate analysis.

"Hey, John do you have a few minutes? I need to discuss something with you that might impact our budget process this year."

"Sure Michael, come on into my office and tell me what the issue is."

"Well, we've done our annual utility rate analysis and it looks like we will need to increase our rates about 10% to meet the debt service coverage ratio. You may recall the principal payments increase significantly next year and this is affecting the coverage calculation."

"Michael, there is no way I can send a rate increase request to the council this year. They aren't too happy with my performance right now and the nail in my coffin might be this increase in utility rates you think we need."

"John, I can appreciate the position you are in but I don't simply 'think' we need a rate increase. The analysis is solid and the additional revenue is needed to cover the increased principal requirements. This is not something we can ignore."

"Well, Michael, I guess this means you will have to find a way to make the numbers work because I will not be taking a rate increase request to the council this year."

Michael returns to his office where he finds Brandon waiting for him.

"I can tell by the look on your face and the clenched fists that things must not have gone well with John."

"Yeah, Brandon, I guess you could say that. He let me know in no uncertain terms he will not take a rate increase to the council this year and I will have to make the numbers work. Your work on the analysis was great by the way. There wasn't anything you omitted even though I wish you had forgotten about the increased principal requirements."

"Thanks, Michael. Let me know if there is anything I can do to help with this."

"Sure thing, Brandon. Hey, I don't recall seeing the county's capacity payment in your analysis. Maybe it could be the thing we need to spin the numbers in our favor."

"Well, I don't think we can because the debt agreement requires us to put capacity payments in a debt service reserve."

"Darn, I forgot about the reserve requirement. Anyway, you still did a great job, Brandon."

After Brandon leaves his office, Michael continues to think about the county's capacity payment and if it would affect Brandon's rate analysis.

"Note to self, run Brandon's numbers with the county's capacity payment and see if it makes the numbers work."

A few days later, Brandon meets with Michael to go over the draft of the quarterly reports to the bond trustee and the rating agencies.

"Michael, I hate to be the bearer of bad news again but we have an issue with the accounts receivable aging for the plant revenues."

"You know, Brandon, if your father wasn't one of my fraternity brothers I'm not sure I would like you at this very minute. Just kidding—your job is safe regardless of what bad news you bear."

"Uh, thanks, Michael."

"All right, tell me about this aging issue we seem to have."

"Everyone in the city knows the big timeshare resort out at the base of the mountain is having some cash flow problems because of the big expansion they did a few years ago. Apparently, their cash flow issues are resulting in more than staff layoffs and reduced hours in the restaurants and bars. Until six months ago, they were paying their utility bills by the due date but their payments have been later and later over the last six months. They are one of our largest customers and their late payments are affecting the 30-day receivables."

"Well, Brandon this is an issue. How far off are we from the required ratios?"

"The 30-day receivables for the quarter are only at 70% and the 60-day accounts are at 20%. I guess the resort doesn't want us to cut off their power because they have managed to pay us within the 60-day cutoff period."

"Thank goodness for small miracles, I guess. Do you still keep these files on the departmental server, Brandon? I'd like to go through things before I sign off on sending the reports to the rating agencies and trustee."

"Yes, the files are still on the server. Let me know if you have any questions or need any help with things."

"Sure thing, Brandon."

The next evening, Michael works late to review the quarterly reports and underlying information. Muttering to himself, Michael says:

"There has to be something I can do to these numbers to make them work. Wait a minute, all I need is the 30-day balances to be 80% of receivables. Let's see, I could increase the 30-day accounts or decrease the 60-day and over accounts or a little bit of both. What makes more sense and is something eagle eye Brandon won't notice? I've got it!"

Michael goes into the utility billing system and writes off several larger 90-day and over 90-day customer balances on accounts where the post office has returned the bills to the city as undeliverable. He reruns the aging reports, but these changes do not bring the 30-day accounts to 80%. Still muttering, Michael says:

"I can't really write off any many more accounts because there are no more 'missing' customers. How can I get current account balances in a fully integrated utility billing system? This may sound crazy but what if I set up new customers and then do manual current period bills for them? No, Brandon would notice the increased amounts in a heartbeat. Maybe . . . yes, this will work!"

Michael uses the manual billing option to recreate the resort's bill for the prior month as a current month bill. To avoid a duplicate bill, Michael uses the manual override function to delete the resort's original bill for the prior month. Doing this does not affect the revenue and receivable balances in the control accounts but it does in effect reclassify the resort's prior month bill as a 30-day receivable. Michael reruns the aging reports and the aging is in line with the amounts specified in the bond covenants. He prints hard copies of the aging report for inclusion in the quarterly bond reporting package.

The next morning Brandon sees a haggard looking Michael in the break room.

"Mornin', Michael. It looks like you had a late night. I hope you had a good time."

"Not hardly. I was here late last night working on the aging issue you dumped on me yesterday. It was all for the good as I waved my magic wand and was able to get things where they need to be for the quarter. By the way, I transmitted the e-copy of the reporting package last night and dropped off the hard copies at the Post Office on my way in this morning."

"Wow, I'm not sure what you did but I hope it wasn't illegal! Just kidding."

"Don't worry, Brandon. Everything was on the up-and-up, which is why I get the big bucks."

John Rogers, the city manager, walks in and sees Michael and Brandon talking.

"I sure hope you two are talking about the rate analysis numbers. Michael, when can we talk about this again?"

"I've got some time right now if you want to hear my good news."

"Great! I've got two calls with council members right now but I should be finished with them in an hour. I'll stop by your office when I finish, if this works for you."

"I'll see you in an hour then, John."

Brandon looks at Michael in disbelief and says:

"What did I miss in the analysis? You told me it was great. I realize John wasn't going to support a rate increase next year but I don't know how he can avoid it based on the analysis."

"Brandon, there are times when you have to get creative and be a little flexible and this is one of those times. Follow me to my office and I'll explain things."

A few minutes later Michael is telling Brandon about the changes he made to the rate analysis.

"All right, Brandon, what I am about to tell you stays in this room. First thing I did was eliminate the capitalized interest we had on the books because GASB Statement No. 89 eliminates it for proprietary funds. This means it will decrease our amortization expense going forward, which creates a positive impact on the rate analysis."

"Wait a minute, Michael, the requirements in Statement No. 89 are to be applied prospectively, which means we won't be able to eliminate what we have on the books now."

"Potato, potahto. Do you think anyone will really even know the standards have changed much less as to how? Whether you agree or not, I'm eliminating the capitalized interest for purposes of the rate analysis. It's only a rate analysis for goodness sake! I'm not sure I want to tell you about the other assumption I made since you don't seem to agree with my interpretation of Statement No. 89."

"It's all right, Michael. Everyone is entitled to their opinion. Go ahead and finish telling me what you did."

"You know how the bond agreement requires us to deposit any capacity payments in the debt service fund? Well, since the purpose of the rate analysis is to determine if current rates are sufficient to meet the debt service ratio, I decided to cast the analysis using the cash basis rather than the accrual basis. By using this approach, I can justify using the capacity payments as 'cash' available for debt service. Using this approach, the numbers tell a totally different story than yours do."

"Michael, while I can admire your creativity, I cannot agree with using the cash approach for the rate analysis. The reason for the annual rate analysis is also to ensure current rates will provide sufficient revenues to meet the coverage ratio at the end of the year. The bond agreement requires the annual debt service coverage ratio be based on the audited GAAP financial statements. Using the cash basis for the rate analysis apparently eliminates the need for a rate increase but it won't help us at the end of the year if we don't meet the coverage ratio. Do you really want to risk defaulting on the bonds next year?"

Looking straight at Brandon, Michael says:

"Let me explain the org chart to you, Brandon. You are the accounting manager, not the finance director, and the buck does not stop with you; it stops with me.

"But Michael, you accessed the rate analysis last and it will have your electronic signature on it."

"No, Brandon, it won't because I accessed it using your login and password. You shouldn't keep that password book in your top desk drawer. By the way, if you mention this conversion to anyone and I am asked about it later, I will deny this conversation. I will also put full responsibility for the rate analysis totally on you and simply cop to not having reviewed it as well as I should have. While I may suffer some reputational damage and lose credibility with the council and John, you *will* lose your job."

"You're kidding me, right? I am so out of here."

Knowledge check

3. Which is accurate of Jackson City?

    a. The city and the trustee for the bonds entered into two covenants with respect to the utility revenue bonds.

    b. Should any of the covenants related to the utility bonds be violated, the bonds may be called by the trustee.

    c. The city is not required to have audited financial statements.

    d. The accounting manager manipulated utility billing and collection records in the current year in order to meet bond covenants.

Exercises

1. Do any of the situations described in this case study represent fraud? If so, what situations and how did they occur?

2. What preliminary audit procedures might have detected this situation?

3. What other audit procedures might have detected this situation?

4. If you were the auditor and discovered this situation, would you communicate this situation to others? If so, to whom? How might this situation affect any planned reliance on internal controls?

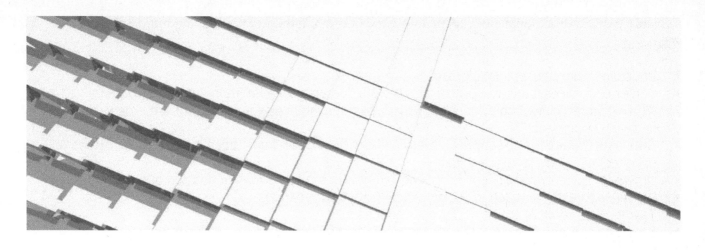

Case 2: Misappropriation of Assets

Learning objectives

- Identify how procurement policies of a fictitious governmental organization can be circumvented and lead to possible fraud.

- Determine the effect technical expertise plays in the development and execution of procurement policies in a fictitious governmental organization.

Before we start

Governmental organizations typically focus controls more on cash receipts than on cash disbursements in order to prevent, deter, or detect the misappropriation of cash. Fraud schemes to misappropriate cash also can occur when an entity pays for goods or services it does not receive. Factors contributing to this particular situation include the following:

- Highly technical transactions
- Insufficient number of trained personnel
- Lack of personnel, or lack of trained personnel, in support functions

© 2019 Association of International Certified Professional Accountants. All rights reserved.   2-1

Typical situations that might indicate the existence of procurement or contracting fraud include the following:

- Unusual vendor names and addresses
- Copies of invoices, purchase orders, or receiving documents rather than original documents
- Missing paper or electronic supporting documentation such as invoices, purchase orders, or receiving documents
- Orders for materials and supplies already on hand in sufficient quantities, scheduled for disposal, or no longer used due to obsolescence
- Orders for materials and supplies not consistent with the operations or mission of the organization
- Delivery addresses not part of the purchaser's physical locations
- Payments to vendors not on approved vendor lists
- Signature of management or supervisory personnel on documents typically signed by subordinate personnel
- Suppliers and contractors receiving significant amounts of business from the organization

Background

Riverside is a primarily blue-collar small city located in a major metropolitan area. It borders the county seat, St. Charles. Most of the city's residents are retired or work outside the city in other areas of the metropolitan area. Although the metropolitan area's population has increased significantly over the last 20 years, Riverside's population has steadily declined. The decline in population has reduced the need for city services; and, as a result, the city employs about half as many people as it did 20 years ago. Four years ago, the city hired the director of St. Charles' planning department as its city manager.

Riverside has limited personnel in the accounting and information technology (IT) functions, both of which report to the city manager. The accounting function is led by an accounting manager who supervises one accounting clerk and one utility clerk. In the IT function there is only one position, the IT manager position. Both the accounting manager and the utility clerk have worked for the city since they graduated from high school 50 years ago. The accounting clerk was hired two years ago upon graduation from the region's premier university.

When the city's current financial management system was installed four years ago, it became evident to the accounting manager and city manager an IT manager was needed. The salary advertised for the position was far less than market salaries for similar positions in the area and very few qualified individuals applied for the job. After advertising the position for almost a year, the city hired a recent information systems graduate from a small out-of-state college. The IT manager is responsible for overseeing operation of the financial management system and for administering the city's internal and external networks, website, and social media.

Knowledge check

1. Which is accurate of Riverside?

    a. Riverside is located in a rural area.
    b. Riverside is a growing city.
    c. The majority of the residents of Riverside work in Riverside.
    d. Riverside employees about half the number of people it did 20 years ago.

2. Which is **not** accurate of Riverside's IT function?

    a. The IT manager position was created four years ago.
    b. Very few individuals applied for the IT manager position when it was first advertised.
    c. The IT manager graduated from the area's premier university.
    d. The IT manager position is responsible for overseeing operation of the financial management system and for administering the city's internal and external network, website, and social media.

The case

The following conversation occurs between Accounting Clerk Savanah Zhang and IT Manager Justin Barnes as they are walking into city hall early on a Monday morning. They are discussing Utility Clerk Gloria Elker and Accounting Manager Mercedes Slater.

"Hi there, Justin. What brings you in this early on a Monday morning?"

"Oh, hi there yourself, Savanah. I'm usually in this early to make sure everything is all good for you, Mercedes, and Gloria. What's in the bakery box?"

"It's Ms. Slater's 50-year work anniversary today and we're celebrating with her favorite yellow cake with chocolate frosting. Yum, yum."

"I can't believe Battle-Ax Mercedes has worked here 50 years. You would think she would have retired by now along with crazy Gloria."

"Wait a minute there, Justin. That's a terrible name for Mercedes, and Gloria is not crazy. She may have five cats and be as old as Mercedes but it doesn't make her crazy. In fact, I think she's one of the least crazy people I know. I hate to think what will happen when she and Mercedes decide to retire, though. Thank goodness both of them still love what they do here at the city."

"Whatever. Have a great day, Savanah."

Justin walks down the hall to his office while Savanah goes into the breakroom to put Mercedes's cake in the refrigerator. As she is getting her desk ready for the day, Savanah mutters:

"I was going to ask Justin what was up with the sweet ride I saw him get out of this morning but, nooooo, he couldn't be bothered to hang with me much past the door."

"What's that, Savanah?"

"Oops, hi Mercedes. I didn't realize you were already here. Sorry, I was talking to myself and thinking about Justin's car."

"What car? He drives a 10-year-old F150 his daddy passed down to him."

"Well, I don't know about the F150, but the car he got out of this morning was some sporty little number. I couldn't tell you what make or model, but it was definitely new, or new to him, because it had a temporary license tag. It was a color somewhat like lapis lazuli."

Utility Clerk Gloria Elker walks in saying:

"Who's lazy, Savanah, Justin? Oh, hi Mercedes. How was the weekend with the grandkids?"

"Holy buckets, Gloria, are your hearing aids turned on? She said lapis lazuli, which is apparently a color. I'm not sure what color it is but it sounds exotic. Oh, yes, the grandkids were wild, but I loved every minute they were with me."

"You guys are nuts. Lapis lazuli is my favorite shade of blue and the color of Justin's new car."

"Well, well, well. Lazy Justin got a new car. I guess he's too good for a beat-up 10-year-old F150 now that he is a homeowner in the ritzy new condo building in uptown St. Charles. Where is he getting the money for all of these things, anyway?" *Whispering, Gloria says to Savanah,* "Did you remember the surprise?"

"Gloria, stop whispering. You two talked about the cake every time I turned my back last week."

"Mercedes, you are no fun, but we should have known it would be impossible to pull one over on you. Gloria, I'll get the cake if you'll call everyone in to wish Mercedes a happy work anniversary."

"Sure thing, Savanah."

A few days later Savanah is processing invoices for payment while Gloria is getting ready to print utility bills.

"Savanah, I'll be done with printing the bills in about 30 minutes. Do you want to go to lunch together? Mercedes is working through lunch because she needs to leave early for a dental appointment. She said she would hold down the fort while we're gone."

"It sounds great, Gloria, but I have a ton of invoices to enter by noon tomorrow if I'm going to get checks in the mail Friday. You know these crazy vendors we use always want to get paid on time. What's up with that, anyway?"

"How about I bring you something back from Blossoms? Isn't their strawberry salad one of your favorites?"

"Would you? By the time you get back, I should be able to sneak 15 minutes in the breakroom to eat it. Gloria, you always know everything going around town. Have you heard if we have a new tech shop in town? Justin sent in paperwork to set up a new vendor and I haven't heard of them."

"I haven't heard anything about a new tech shop coming into town, but I haven't talked to my cousin at the Chamber lately."

"No problem. I'll see what I can find out about them but there may not be much if they've only been in business a short while."

Later in the afternoon while Savanah is eating lunch in the break room, she sees Justin walking to his car with several boxes and his laptop bag. City manager, Grant Martin, walks in while she is there.

"I wonder where he's going with those boxes. He's got his laptop, which makes it look like he's heading home for the day. A six-hour workday must be nice."

"Who are you talking to, Savanah?"

"Oh dear. Hi, Grant. I hate to admit it but I'm talking to myself. I'd like to say I picked up the habit from Gloria and Mercedes but I've talked to myself for as long as I can remember."

"What is it they say, it's when you answer yourself you have to worry. Isn't it a bit late to be eating lunch?"

"I guess it is, but I need to get everything entered by noon tomorrow for the weekly check run. I'm taking a short lunch to make sure I have time to get everything done on time."

"All of you in accounting work too hard for what the city pays you. I wish I could tell you things would get better, but I'd be lying. It's no secret next year is going to be tighter than this year as everyone knows we haven't had any new construction or any commercial growth for almost three years."

"Funny thing. Justin gave me paperwork today for a new IT shop in town, which could mean things are about to get better. As for next budget year, you might want to mention this to him as his IT budget has increased dramatically since I started here two years ago. I seem to process more invoices for IT than I do for any other department, including the police department!"

"I realize we spend a lot on IT, but Justin has a strategic plan for our IT future and it apparently does not come cheap."

"Well, the buck stops with you, Grant. I sure wouldn't want your job."

"Some days I don't want it either, Savanah. See you later and don't work too late."

The next morning Savanah is reviewing the accounts payable edit report while Gloria is sorting utility bills into carrier routes for mailing.

"Gloria, could you look at something for me?"

"Sure, Savanah. What do you need?"

"Yesterday when I was in the breakroom eating my very late lunch—thank you again for bringing me the salad—Grant came in and we talked for a bit. He mentioned next year is going to be tighter than this year. I was thinking last night on my way home about Justin and all of his spending. I couldn't wait to get in this morning to look at a few things in this week's check run that bothered me yesterday."

"Gloria, look at these invoices Justin submitted for payment this week. Do you know what any of this stuff is? He's coded this invoice to computer supplies in the police, fire, and public works departments. This invoice here is coded to computer parts and he charged it to his department. How do we know these are even computer parts, much less computer parts we need?"

"I don't know, Savanah. We've always taken Justin's word for these things. When I helped out with AP before we hired you, I used to think the same thing. Doing two jobs every day didn't leave me much time to worry about it though."

"What are you two up to now? You already had an anniversary cake for me. What's next—a recognition dinner?"

"No, Mercedes, the cake was all we had up our sleeves. I'm showing Gloria some of Justin's invoices which are in this week's check run. Here, let me show you too and see what you think."

Savanah shows the invoices to Mercedes and points out what she and Gloria discussed.

"This is all pretty interesting, Savanah. Are there any other invoices like this?"

"I'm not sure, Mercedes, but I wouldn't mind working late to see what I can find."

"You do that but don't stay too late. Life is yours to enjoy at your age. I don't want to be the reason you burn out before you're 30."

"No worries there, Mercedes. If I get into things can I keep looking? I really don't mind staying late or coming in this weekend."

"I don't have a problem with it but please don't work too late. If you do, call Dispatch and have someone come over to escort you to your car."

"Yes, Mom."

Over the next two weeks, Savanah looks into all amounts Justin charged departments and his IT function for anything technology related. She also uses the Internet to check out vendors she isn't familiar with and those Justin requested to be added to the approved vendor list during his four-year tenure. During her investigation she noted a number of invoices were paid over a three-year period to two vendors for "consulting services." When invoice details were sparse, she used the Internet to determine the purpose of the various parts listed on the invoices. She noted five vendors supplied "computer parts" to the city but never provided any supporting documentation for the amounts invoiced.

After two weeks, Savanah meets with Mercedes in her office to discuss what she found in her investigation.

"I'm looking forward to hearing what you have to report Savanah. For the record, I am not pleased with the amount of time you spent investigating instead of enjoying yourself. You are too young to be spending all of your free time at work."

"Mercedes, it's really all right. It's especially all right because what I found makes everything worth all the extra hours. I'll send you copies of everything I have when we're finished here if you want them."

"This sounds ominous, Savanah. What did you find exactly?"

"Here is a summary of my findings and I have the backup documentation with me if you would like to see it as well."

"It's all right, Savanah. The summary is fine for now."

"If you look at the summary, you'll see we paid five vendors over $250,000 for 'computer parts' or 'computer supplies.' These five vendors were set up at Justin's request over the last four years. I find it odd that there are no receiving reports for any of the invoices from these five vendors. In fact, the only supporting documentation for any payment is the purchase order and invoice, both of which Justin approved. I looked at all of the invoices to see who ordered the parts and in every single case it was Justin, even when the parts were charged to another department. Because we paid these vendors a significant amount of money, I called all of them to ask what some of the parts were. Almost all of the parts we paid for are for types of computers and other hardware we don't use at the city."

"What are you saying, Savanah?"

"I don't know where the parts are or what Justin did with them, assuming he received them, which isn't a fact since there are no receiving reports. Justin ordered them and if they aren't compatible with our city hardware, I can only think Justin ordered them for personal purposes. Maybe he has a computer business on the side or maybe he sells the parts on Amazon, eBay, or Craig's List. I don't know anything for sure other than things look suspicious."

"What else did you find, Savanah?"

"We paid two vendors $75,000 each for 'consulting services' and I can't find any evidence the vendors even exist. The invoices look legit, but the vendors are ghosts. I searched the Internet, white and yellow pages, chambers of commerce in the cities the invoices indicate they're located in, as well as the Better Business Bureau. I called the phone numbers we have on file for them in our vendor master file and they are not in service. None of the invoices indicate a physical address, only a post office box, which means I couldn't use Google Maps to find them."

"Oh dear, even I can see where this is going. Are you saying what I think you're saying, Savanah?"

"If you think I'm saying Justin looks to have scammed the city out of $150,000, then yes, this is what I'm saying."

"Let me think about this tonight and we'll talk again tomorrow."

"Sure thing, Mercedes."

"Before you go, do you have a few minutes to look at something with me?"

"Sure."

"Pull your chair up to my desk since everything is on my computer."

"Wow, you've got a ton of screens open right now!"

"Bear with me while I go through them with you. For the last six months, the bank recs have been a bit off. Every month there seems to be a lag between the dates the state says it processes our electronic funds transfers, or EFTs, and the dates they are hitting the bank. With cash being as tight as it is, I monitor the bank balances daily and especially on payroll weeks. The last thing I need is to bounce employee paychecks!"

"Switch places with me Mercedes so I can see look at all the screens."

A few minutes later Savanah looks at Mercedes and sighs.

"I'm not sure why, but there is a difference in the dates, and it seems as if most months the lag is five days. Have you called the bank or the state about it?"

"Not yet because I needed to have another set of eyes look at things. If you still have time, let's call them now."

After spending 20 minutes on the phone with the state department of revenue and the city's banking representative, Mercedes learns the bank routing number and the account number the state is using for the EFTs are not correct. She also learns the bank information for the incoming EFTs is likewise not correct. The bank sends Mercedes a copy of a memo authorizing the change to the bank's EFT information.

"I wish the bank would hurry up and send me the memo. The last time I made any changes was 10 years ago when the city switched banks. I am the only one authorized to make changes to either the state or bank EFT information . . . oh dear. Two years ago, I was out on disability for six weeks when I had my back surgery. We added Justin to the list in case anything came up when I was out, but he told me nothing did. Do you think, no certainly not . . . "

"Mercedes, you have a new message and it's from the bank."

"Move over and let me open the message and print the attachment."

Mercedes and Savanah both look at the memo sent from the bank.

"That little slimy-faced, son of a fraudster, snit. Do you see this Savanah? Look at this! Justin sent this memo to the bank the first week I was out of commission. Why would he do it and what are these account numbers? Let me pull up our account information on file with the department of revenue and see what routing and account numbers are on file."

"Well I'll be . . . the account information for the outgoing state EFTs is the same as the account information on file with the bank for the incoming EFT but neither are city account numbers. Trust me, after all these years, I know our account numbers by sight. Looks like the bank information was changed, thanks to Mr. Barnes. What do you think is going on Savanah?"`

"This may sound crazy, Mercedes, but what if Justin is routing the state EFTs to an account he controls and is in his name? If I had to guess, I'd say he lets the funds sit in this personal account of his for a few days while he earns some interest before he transfers money from it to the city's account at the bank."

"Savanah, I think you may be on to something. I have never had a good feeling about Justin but couldn't put my finger on why. Everyone around city hall knows I'm not a fan and now it seems I've had good reason not to like him."

"Mercedes, I think you need to take this to Grant as soon as possible and let him decide what needs to be done. This is way above both our pay grades."

"Why don't you pull together a memo under my name summarizing your investigation and what we learned this afternoon? After I review it and your other documentation, I'll let you discuss it with Grant."

"No, Mercedes, you need to be the one to discuss this with Grant."

"Savanah, it will be a lot better if the messenger is someone without a known grudge against the apparent fraudster."

"I see your point and I'll do it, but I still think you should be the one to discuss things with Grant."

The following discussion takes place in the office of the city manager, Grant Martin, one week later.

"Hi, Savanah. I was expecting to meet with Mercedes."

"I know and she sends her apologies. Based on what we will be talking about, Mercedes thought it best you hear it from me. It concerns Justin and she has never really hidden how she feels about him. She thought you might be more receptive to listening if it came from me because I don't have any issues with Justin. At least I didn't until a few weeks ago."

"Well, I am certainly intrigued, Savanah. You have my undivided attention."

Over the next 15 minutes, Savanah explains her analysis to Grant as well as what she and Mercedes learned about the EFTs from the state to the bank.

"Savanah, you and Mercedes have done a great analysis here and I'm having a hard time believing what I think I'm seeing. What prompted you to do your analysis anyway?"

"Well, it all started last month when I walked in with Justin and noticed his new lapis lazuli sports car in the parking lot . . . "

"Lapis what?"

"It's a gorgeous deep blue color and my favorite shade of blue, which is probably why I noticed it."

"All right, finish what you were saying before I interrupted you."

"Umm, yes. It all started when I saw his new car. When I mentioned it to Gloria and Mercedes, Gloria mentioned Justin having bought a condo over in the new upscale community in St. Charles. This got me to thinking about other things such as the designer labels Justin wears and how he vacations in places no one I know can afford. He has season tickets for both the basketball and soccer teams, and he travels to some of their away games. This lifestyle doesn't make sense with what I know he makes. Don't look at me like that. I know what he makes because I enter pay changes in the human resources system. Besides, it's public record."

"You make a pretty convincing argument for a lavish lifestyle and even I know this is a fraud indicator. Have you or Mercedes talked to our auditors about this? I know the St. Charles auditors talked to employees all over the city about where they thought fraud might be occurring or if they thought they worked with honest people."

"In the two audits I have been through the auditors only talked to me, Mercedes, and Gloria and one of the department heads. All of us in accounting work closely with the auditors but we've been hesitant to call them about this. I told Mercedes we needed to discuss it with you first and she agreed."

"There is one more thing Mercedes discovered late yesterday, which isn't discussed in her memo. Mercedes spent some time going over the state EFTs we received since Justin changed the account number information. She finished her analysis right before our meeting. You can look at it, but the bottom line is there are differences between several of the EFT amounts the state says they sent and what was ultimately transferred to our bank account. The only time the amounts differed was the six-week period Mercedes was out recovering from her back surgery. It looks like the bank received $25,000 less than what the state transferred to us during this time."

"All right, Savanah. You and Mercedes have given me a lot to think about and I appreciate your candor and courage in coming forward. Tell Mercedes I'm going to look into things. I don't think I need to ask you to keep this conversation between the two of us, do I?"

"No, Grant. Let me know if you need any additional information."

Exercises

1. What type of controls could be put in place to deter procurement-related fraud such as suspected in this case?

2. What type of centralized internal controls and procedures would be appropriate to determine if this type of situation was occurring?

3. What type of decentralized internal controls and procedures would be appropriate to determine if this type of situation was occurring?

4. What type of audit procedures might be appropriate to determine if this type of situation was occurring?

5. What would you do if you were the city manager and why?

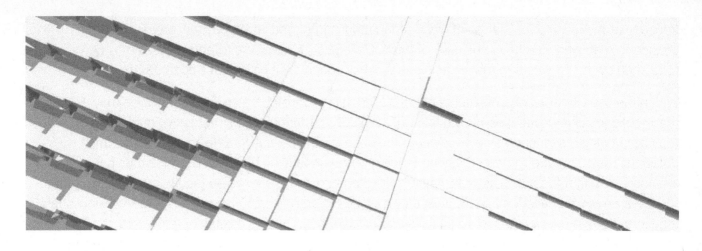

Chapter 3

Case 3: Management Override

Learning objectives

- Identify how the president of a fictitious government university can put pressure on staff to do things that may not appear to be in the public interest.

- Identify how management override of internal controls can lead to possible fraud in a fictitious government college.

Before we start

The higher education environment is one in which numerous highly degreed and credentialed academicians and professionals work within a somewhat hierarchical environment. In some cases, persons in the highest positions in the organization may not have the necessary business acumen to lead an institution to prominence or to hire individuals who could. Most colleges and universities have a very structured organizational chart that is steeped in history and tradition rather than what works best to run the "business" of higher education.

At the top of most organizational charts is the president of the college or university who answers, typically, only to the board of trustees. From a fraud perspective, if the presidential "tone at the top" is one of zero tolerance and fraudsters are promptly disciplined, employees may be less likely to commit fraud. Fostering a positive and open work environment at all levels of the organization also helps in preventing, detecting, and deterring fraud.

Because of the hierarchical nature of higher education institutions, staff may feel pressure from the president to do whatever he or she asks of them. College or university level committees may be pressured by the president to make decisions that will support the president's positions.

Within the departmental organizational structure, additional formal or informal hierarchies may exist. In many colleges and universities, individuals with degrees, credentials, and impressive publishing records may be in positions of leadership or power at the department, college, or university level. As such, decisions may be made without an understanding of the underlying business purpose thus negating any intended oversight function. Likewise, when highly degreed and credentialed faculty are awarded grants for research or other academic purposes, they may be resistant to other seemingly low-level individuals requiring them to follow established policies and procedures. The expression "herding cats" is often used to describe the process of getting these individuals to act within policy norms or to reach a decision.

Related to the tone at the top of a governmental college or university is the attitude of the board of trustees with respect to management's override of existing internal controls. Management override most often occurs in the following areas:

- Journal entries
- Estimates
- Business rationale for transactions
    - Bribes and kickbacks
    - Billing schemes

Background

Upstate College is a small state college in the northeast United States and has been in existence for more than 100 years. It is governed by a 15-member board of trustees who answer to the state legislature. Over the past 10 years, the college has been experiencing financial difficulties primarily because they are unable to attract high-quality faculty.

The lack of highly qualified faculty has resulted in a significant decrease in grant funding and an exodus of many of the remaining highly qualified faculty. Without a significant level of grant funding, the college has less to spend on education, maintenance of facilities, and support staff. The board of trustees is reluctant to request an increase in tuition and fee levels from the legislature because they fear it will have a negative effect on student recruitment and enrollment.

These issues have also resulted in the college being unable to meet performance benchmarks imposed on them by the state legislature. Benchmarks are established for every college and university in the state university system and relate to such things as enrollment, grant funding, faculty publications, and student academic achievement. Due to increasing pressure by the state legislature on the college's board of trustees, the board fired its long-time president and is currently in the process of hiring a new president.

Knowledge check

1. Which is accurate of Upstate College?

    a. Upstate College is a small state college in the northeast United States.
    b. Upstate College is in good financial condition.
    c. There are 10 members on the board of trustees.
    d. The college has no problem attracting and hiring highly qualified faculty.

The case

The following exchange takes place during a phone call between Tuan Nguyen, personnel director, and Nelson Odom, chair of the board of trustees.

"Listen here, Tuan, we need to move this president selection process along a lot faster than we are now. I realize we haven't had many applicants, and not many of those look like what we need, but we need to step on the gas here. We really need the position filled by the start of summer if we want the new president to be up to speed when classes start."

"With all due respect, Mr. Chairman, the application deadline has been extended three times, which is the main reason the process is six months behind schedule. Even if you selected someone tomorrow we would still need another six to eight weeks to conduct the background checks, interview references, and the other due diligence required under our policies."

"I don't want to hear excuses, Tuan. When we get you a name, I want you to work night and day to get things done. Are we clear here?"

"Absolutely, sir."

Two months later Tuan Nguyen receives another call from Nelson Odom.

"Great news, Tuan. We finally found us a president and she looks like a real go-getter. Her name is Cathryn Johnson and she's from some tiny college in upstate Minnesota. I'm sending you her resume and personal information by courier even as we speak. Let's get everything done and get her here by the middle of May."

"Sir, the last time we talked I reminded you it would take us six to eight weeks to complete the due diligence. The middle of May is five weeks from now and I'm not sure all the paperwork will be done by then."

"And I told *you*, Tuan, the last time we talked I wanted you to work night and day to get things done once we had a name. Let's get this done and get it done ASAP."

"Mr. Chairman, state and college policies prohibit you from extending a permanent offer of employment until all the paperwork is in hand. However, you can extend a conditional offer of employment contingent upon everything being in order. I can get our standard conditional offer of employment letter to you this afternoon."

"Now that's the team spirit I like to see. Goodbye, Tuan."

"Goodbye Mr. Chairman."

Muttering, Tuan says:

I'm not sure I'd want to pack up and move without a firm employment offer but then again, I'm not looking at being a college president."

The following phone call takes place three weeks later.

"I'm sorry Mr. Chairman but I don't have any more information to report today than I did two days ago. The FBI background test is still in process even though we put a rush status on it, her drug test is back, we are still checking references, and we are still trying to interview former faculty and students. We are having a very difficult time finding former colleagues and students willing to talk with us, sir."

"What in the blazes are you doing talking to former faculty and students? If this is slowing down the process, then you best forget about doing it."

"With all due respect, sir, interviewing former faculty and students is a required due diligence procedure under the college's recruitment and hiring policies. The policy has been in place 15 years and has provided us with valuable insights in the past. We learn things from these interviews about a person we would never find through a background check or by checking references."

"I'm telling you right now, Tuan, to drop these interviews. If the FBI background check comes in this week then I'm calling the process done. I don't care if we have references or not. We need to get her here now, not later."

"Mr. Chairman, I understand your frustration, but I am not comfortable with circumventing our controls. My name is on the letterhead of this department and I take my responsibilities very seriously. If you insist on stopping the process, I can't stop you unless I go to the board. Since you are the chair, I'm pretty sure going to the board for support will be a wasted effort."

"You're right about that, Tuan. When I say jump, all 14 of them ask how high. Now get this paperwork mess wrapped up this week."

"Yes, sir."

Knowledge check

2. Which is accurate of Upstate College?

    a. Tuan Nguyen is the chairman of the board of trustees.
    b. Upstate College does not conduct FBI background checks.
    c. Tuan Nguyen is the personnel director for Upstate College.
    d. The board wishes the president to be in place by mid-September.

---

3. Which is accurate of Upstate College?

    a. The new president is from a college in Missouri.
    b. The chairman of the board believes the new president is not a self-starter.
    c. The new president is from a large college in Minnesota.
    d. Cathryn Johnson is the new president.

Over the next few days, Tuan receives the FBI background check, which is fine, but he also receives interview reports that are concerning. In addition, only two of the five professional references provided information when asked. In three of the interviews of former faculty and staff, the interviewers noted the individuals were nervous and asked to remain anonymous. The gist of what all three told the interviewers was Cathryn Johnson was a difficult person to work with and she tended to intimidate people until she got her way.

Tuan calls Chairman Nelson Odom, to give him a status report.

"Tell me you have good news, Tuan. We need to start planning the press conferences and receptions for our new president and the sooner she is here to provide input, the better."

"I recall from our conversation a few days ago you wanted me to circumvent our procedures and wrap up the due diligence as soon as we received the FBI background check, which we did two days ago. Unfortunately, there are only three interviews with former faculty and students and they aren't particularly positive. In fact, their comments lead me to believe our candidate may not fit in well with our culture here at Upstate."

"Last time I checked, Tuan, you only had a master's degree in organizational psychology not a Ph.D. In my book this means your opinion isn't worth squat. Besides, I've met Cathy and spent quite a bit of time with her and I think she's a great fit. Write your report and get me a formal offer letter for her by end of business today."

"Yes, sir."

Four months later, President Cathryn Johnson has moved into the college-provided house and ordered her college-provided sport utility vehicle. Plans are underway for her "inauguration" as president in three weeks. The following conversation occurs between President Johnson and Patrick Crowley, college chief financial officer.

"Pat, I need you to transfer money into my discretionary account to cover some of my inauguration expenses."

"Dr. Johnson, please. I've asked you before to call me by my given name, which is Patrick. As for transferring funds, there are no more available funds to transfer for the event. The budget for all of your welcoming events was $50,000 and with the transfer of $15,000 last week the budget is now zero. How much do you need, anyway?"

"All right, *Patrick*, I need $25,000. Premier caterers in this town don't come cheap and I only want top-shelf liquor served. The $25,000 may not even cover what I need."

"President Johnson, that's $40,000 I know of for this event and it amounts to more than the total discretionary fund budgeted for the last eight years! Please remember that although you control the discretionary fund, it is supposed to be used to support educational, social, and cultural events as well as programs of the college. Taking a loose interpretation of the fund's purpose, I suppose you could classify your 'inauguration' as a social event, but this means you won't have any funds for the remainder of the budget year. It's only mid-September and you've used your budget, and then some, for the entire year!"

"Patrick! I want you to remember I am the president of this college and what I say goes. If I say jump, you ask how high. Got it?"

"Got it."

After President Odom leaves the finance department, several of the staff stop by to commiserate with Patrick. Trying to be a team player, he reminds everyone the role of the finance function is to support the college, including the president.

Six months later one accounting clerk, Melissa Burns, returns from lunch and goes immediately to Patrick's office.

"Patrick, you are not going to believe what I heard today at lunch."

"I'm sure I won't, Melissa, but why don't you tell me anyway."

"I went to lunch with my friend in the human resources (HR) department and she told me Tuan was fired yesterday. Get this—he was fired while he was at lunch. Apparently, security dumped all of his things in boxes, put the boxes in the hall, and changed the lock on his office door."

"You're right, Melissa, I don't believe this. Tuan is only five years from entering the deferred retirement option plan program and he and his wife are planning to move to Florida when he retires. What happened? Wait a minute, Tuan reports only to the president, which means she is the only one who could fire him."

"Well, I don't know about who reports to who, but I did hear that the president was the one to sign his letter of separation."

"Did this friend of yours with a wealth of information have any idea why Tuan might have been fired?"

"Nothing concrete but he did mention there were several times Tuan disagreed with the president and a few when he wouldn't sign off on hiring someone she recommended. It seems she met with Tuan last week behind closed doors and the staff heard her screaming even with the door closed. No one heard everything the president was screaming about but they heard enough to figure out Tuan might have voiced some reservations about her before she was officially hired."

"This is consistent with some of the stories I have heard around campus about her temper and running over anyone she thinks is standing in her way. Thanks for letting me know about Tuan, Melissa."

Three months later Patrick is reviewing various accounts and getting things together for the annual financial and compliance audits. While reviewing the schedule of capital asset additions, he comes across something unexpected and calls Melissa into his office.

"Melissa, I'm going over things before we hand everything over to the auditors next month and I ran across a few confusing things in the capital asset addition schedule. It took me a while to figure out what I thought I was seeing because there are a number of related items rather than one single item."

"What can I help you with, Patrick?"

"Look at these items I highlighted in yellow. They all seem to be related to renovations at the president's house. I was able to figure out that they related to the renovations because I looked at the underlying invoices and the delivery address. I remember some mention of the board approving a few renovations but the items I highlighted total almost $300,000. I'm not sure what the carrying value of the president's house is but $300,000 sounds like a significant renovation."

"I only process the invoices and verify that the account coding looks appropriate, which means I wouldn't have noticed anything because the items here are spread over six months, it looks like. Do you think the board approved renovations of this magnitude?"

"I couldn't say, Melissa, as I don't attend meetings of the trustees. I'll see if I can get copies of the minutes of the meetings to see exactly what they approved. Look at the items I highlighted here in blue. According to the invoices, all of these were to 'refurbish' the president's office."

"Oh my goodness, Patrick! There are more than $70,000 worth of 'refurbishments' here. I'm not sure what everything is but I see a desk costing $25,000 and wallpaper costing $5,000. Is this something all new presidents get to do?"

"If the board approved it I guess it's something this president was able to do. I'll be looking for the approval of the refurbishments in the minutes as well. I'll let you know if I have any more questions but, in the meantime, Melissa, please keep this between the two of us. I'd hate to see one or both of us get fired because someone might see this as questioning her authority. After all, look what happened to Tuan."

For the next several months, Patrick was too busy with the audit, getting the new budget year started, and drafting the financial statements to further investigate the president's capital asset purchases. In January, Melissa comes into Patrick's office and closes the door.

"Patrick, I know you've been busy the last six months with the year-end close and the new fiscal year, but I ran across something yesterday I thought you might like to know."

"Sure thing, Melissa. What is it?"

"Our conversation before year -end got me to thinking and I've been more vigilant with the items going through capital assets. In fact, I'm doing a monthly analysis of the charges to our capital accounts, but I didn't start doing it until two months ago when things slowed down."

"The monthly analysis is a great idea, Melissa, and starting it four months into the new fiscal year is better than doing it the last month of the year."

"Thanks, Patrick. The thing is, in July we paid the GMC dealership an additional $6,000 over what should have been the state contract amount for 'options' to the president's car."

"What do you mean 'what should have been the state contract price'?"

"According to the purchase contract, the president purchased a luxury model rather than the model on state contract. I did some research and it looks as if the luxury model cost $10,000 more than the state contract model. The $6,000 in options is on top of the contract price."

"Well, the rumors of her lavish spending habits seem to be truer and truer every day. Was there anything else, Melissa?"

"There is one more thing. Did you know the president receives $1,000 each month as a 'car allowance'? My friend in HR mentioned he noticed it when he was getting the non-compensation data ready for entry before they processed W-2s. I thought you might know why we pay the maintenance expenses on her college-owned vehicle if she has a car allowance. Isn't the purpose of a car allowance to help someone pay for the business use of a personal vehicle?"

"I don't think I ever connected the dots until you mentioned it. I wasn't aware of the car allowance, but I did know a college-provided vehicle was part of her contract. I didn't see a car allowance in her contract and I am almost positive I would have noticed it because it doesn't make sense when we provide her a vehicle. This looks like something else to put on my list of things to investigate."

As she leaves Patrick's office, Mellissa says:

"Cheer up, Patrick. You have plenty of time for a forensic investigation every Sunday morning between 2am and 3am!"

Over the next several months, Patrick takes copies and electronic files home with him to avoid working on his investigation in the office. He is unable to obtain copies of the minutes of the board meetings and the college budget committee meetings and doesn't think it wise to request the documents through a public records request. Patrick asks his friend Nathan (Nate) Fox, who is a reporter for a local affiliate of a national network, to make a public records request for the documents. After numerous delays and repeat formal requests, the college provides the documents to Nathan almost four months after his first request. He meets Patrick at a local diner to give him the documents.

"Thanks, Nate. I can't tell you enough how much I appreciate you getting these documents for me."

"No worries, Patrick. Don't forget you promised me an exclusive when you get everything figured out. And a bottle of Gentleman Jack."

"You always did drive a hard bargain, Nate. I should have everything ready to go in less than a month. You better start thinking about how your Pulitzer Prize-winning headline will read."

Patrick is not surprised to find nothing indicating approval of the renovations to the president's house, office refurbishment, upgraded vehicle, or car allowance in the minutes of the board of trustees. What does surprise him are the minutes of the college budget committee meetings. Over the last 18 months, the college budget committee approved a number of transfers from other sources to the president's discretionary fund.

Patrick notes a transfer of over $80,000 from monies set aside by the board for adult and continuing education programs. Another transfer of almost $75,000 was made from the Student Government Association funds. Although the minutes don't capture the tone of the meetings, Patrick concludes the president likely strong-armed the budget committee into approving the transfers.

By the end of the month Patrick's analysis is complete and he meets with Nate Fox to give him the information he will need for his investigative report.

"All right, Nate, these envelopes have copies of everything I looked at as well as my Excel spreadsheet analyses . . ."

"Don't look like you are about to face a firing squad, Nate. I know Excel files give you hives, which is why I have summarized everything in an anonymous memo to you. As I told you when I first reached out to you, my name can't be anywhere near this. If the federal or state auditors open an investigation, I will cooperate in every way possible if I am asked. But for purposes of the 11pm news, I am a ghost."

"I got it, Patrick. Can you at least give me a little hint as to how big this might be?"

"Well, our esteemed president may get away with a lot of what ran through her discretionary account because the board never exercised any control over it even though they had the authority to review the account. What is going to grab headlines is she and her family of five went to Norway and Sweden over the holiday break. They flew first class and stayed in five-star hotels and the college paid 100 percent of the trip for all of them, which came to almost $60,000. You might also want to look into where she bought 500 copies of a book using her advertising budget."

"Who needs 500 copies of one book, Patrick?"

"She does, Nate, because she was listed as the editor of one of the chapters!"

"Wow, this is going to be a fun assignment!"

Exercises

1. Does this case present a type of fraud risk? If so, what type of fraud risk?

2. Which part, if any, of the fraud triangle (pressure, rationalization, opportunity) is represented in this case? Explain your response.

3. What type of preventive or detective controls might have prevented/detected this type of situation?

4. What type of audit procedures could be performed that might detect this situation?

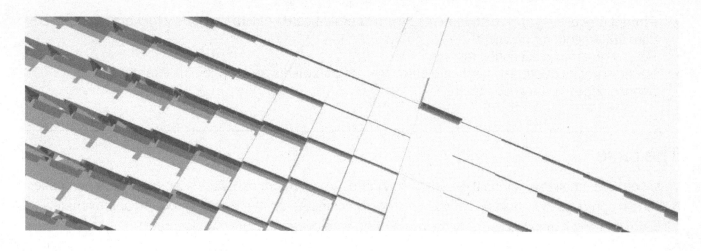

Chapter 4

Case 4: Procurement Cards

Learning objectives

- Identify characteristics of effective procurement card policies for a fictitious governmental organization.

- Determine how procurement card policies can be circumvented and lead to fraud in a fictitious governmental organization.

Before we start

Today, a number of state and local governments use procurement cards to streamline the purchasing and payables cycle associated with relatively small, routine, and frequent purchases of operating supplies. Examples of controls over procurement cards that are effective if properly designed and performed include the following:

- Prohibiting the use of procurement cards for the purchase of gift cards.
- Blocking the cash and counter checks options on all procurement cards.
- Having written policies and procedures relating to the issuance and use of procurement cards.
- Requiring employees with procurement cards to execute a cardholder's agreement prior to being issued a procurement card. The agreement should specifically state the
  - employee's responsibilities with respect to the use of the card.
  - consequences if the procurement card is used fraudulently.
- Requiring the submission of receipts for every item on the procurement card statement and a review of the receipts and statement by a responsible and appropriate party.

- Prompt processing of card statements by procurement card holders and timely forward of approved card statements for payment.
- Review of periodic exception reports.
- Random audits of procurement card purchases or statements (or both) by the internal audit or finance or accounting department.

The case

Wills Ford is a small town along the eastern seaboard. Procurement cards are used for routine purchases by certain approved individuals. The finance department instituted the "P-Card" program approximately 10 years ago and it has become very popular among employees and city management.

Originally, the P-Card program was developed to streamline purchasing of day-to-day and routine purchases for all city departments. The P-Card program also eliminated a lot of time spent by accounts payable personnel in processing numerous small or routine purchases from a large number of vendors. Approximately 50% of the city's non-personnel expenditures are made using procurement cards.

To compensate for the lack of centralized control, the chief financial officer (CFO) developed procedures for all personnel involved directly or indirectly in purchasing through the P-Card program. Selected P-Card policy and program controls are as follows:

City of Wills Ford Selected P-Card policy and program controls
Each department director is allowed to designate which of their staff is to be issued a P-Card. However, only employees at a supervisory level or above are automatically considered eligible for a P-Card.
Employees at less than a supervisory level may be issued a P-Card. In these cases, the department director must prepare a written request stating why the employee needs a P-Card and how he or she will use it. These requests are reviewed and approved by the CFO.
All employees being given P-Card privileges, their immediate supervisor, and their department director sign a P-Card authorization and agreement form. By signing the form, the employee indicates he or she understands all policies and procedures associated with the P-Card program and agrees to adhere to them at all times.
Violation of any P-Card policy or procedure may result in the immediate and permanent suspension of an employee's P-Card privileges by the CFO.
P-Card procedures prohibit the use of an employee's P-Card by anyone other than the employee.
When employment is terminated, an employee's P-Card is returned to his or her immediate supervisor.

City of Wills Ford
Selected P-Card policy and program controls (continued)
Each employee is subject to purchasing limits including maximum daily purchases (number and amount), maximum monthly purchases (number and amount), and maximum per purchase transaction amount. In addition, each employee is limited as to type of merchant based on his or her position, function, and purchasing authority. All dollar and transaction limits, as well as allowable merchant codes, are programmed by the issuing financial institution into the card.
An exception report is electronically transmitted each day to the CFO. The CFO reviews the daily report and sends it to the appropriate department director for review and investigation. Department directors are required to respond to the exception report within five business days.
All purchasing and transaction limits on employee P-Cards are established by their department director and approved by the CFO. Limits may be increased or decreased at the discretion of the appropriate department director and upon approval of the CFO.
Each employee assigned a P-Card is responsible for reconciling his or her monthly statement and attaching the receipts. Employees sign the P-Card statement indicating they have reviewed the purchases and are authorizing them for payment.
An employee's immediate supervisor reviews his or her P-Card statement and all related receipts. The supervisor then approves and signs the monthly P-Card statement and routes it to accounts payable for payment. The supervisor follows up with the employee if any receipts are missing or if any charges appear questionable.
Accounts payable personnel review the P-Card statement for the proper signatures (employee and supervisor) and to determine receipts are attached before it is input for payment.
The CFO reserves the right to review any P-Card statement activity at any time.

Knowledge check

1. Which is accurate of Wills Ford's P-Card program?

    a. Accounts payable personnel review the P-Card statement but do not look for attached receipts.
    b. Employees sign the P-Card statement indicating they have reviewed the purchases and are authorizing them for payment.
    c. Few employees given P-Card privileges sign a P-Card authorization and agreement form.
    d. Employees assigned a P-Card are not responsible for reconciling their monthly statement and attaching the receipts.

2. Which is accurate of Wills Ford's P-Card program?

    a. Employees' immediate supervisors review their P-Card statement and all related receipts.
    b. Supervisors are not responsible for following up with employees if any receipts are missing or if any charges appear questionable.
    c. Employees' immediate supervisors are not required to review their P-Card statements before sending them to accounts payable for payment.
    d. Accounts payable personnel do not review the P-Card statement prior to processing the bill for payment.

3. Which is accurate of Wills Ford's P-Card program?

    a. The CFO reserves the right to review any P-Card statement activity at any time.
    b. An exception report is electronically transmitted each day to the individual P-Card holder.
    c. All dollar and transaction limits, as well as allowable merchant codes, are programmed by accounts payable into the card.
    d. The P-Card authorization and agreement form is signed by only the employee being given P-Card privileges.

The following conversation occurs at 7am as the A shift is taking over from the C shift between A shift patrol officers, Alexander (Alex) Bassett and Alexis Jordan; A shift sergeant, Marvin Templeton; and, C shift sergeant, Dennis Jackson.

Well, looky here. It's Alex all dressed up and nowhere to go and nothing to do. How about I see if I can fix that nothing-to-do thing for you. What do you *want* me to give you to do today, boys?"

"Good morning, Sergeant Templeton. Alexis and I will take whatever assignment you give us today."

"How's it going, Alexander? Have you adjusted to being on the A shift yet?"

"Things are pretty good, Sergeant Jackson. I really appreciate you supporting my transfer from C shift to A shift. My wife is very happy to have me home to help out with our little guy in the evenings."

"Glad to hear it and happy I could do something to help out one of the department's rising stars. How old is your son now, anyway?"

"Zach will be six months next week and he's getting his first tooth. Sarge, do you remember Alexis Jordan? She came over to us from Baytown a few months ago."

"Alexis, this is Sergeant Jackson the backbone of C shift."

"Nice to meet you, Sergeant."

"Good to meet you too, Alexis. Please, call me Sarge like everyone else does. Some of us don't hold on to antiquated ideas about the chain of command like others."

"Sergeant Templeton is glaring at us, Alex. We better get ready for roll call."

As Alex and Alexis are walking to their patrol unit after roll call they see Sergeant Jackson who waves Alex over to talk to him. After a few minutes, Alex returns to the patrol unit.

"What was that all about, Alex?"

"It was nothing, Alexis. Sarge wanted to know if I could run an errand for him this morning since he's exhausted and wants to get home and hit the sack. Mondays aren't usually too busy for us. I kind of feel like I owe him for helping me get my transfer to A shift, so I told him I'd do it. It's not a big deal as Target is on our way to our patrol quadrant."

Later Alex stops at Target and leaves Alexis in the car in case they have a call. He returns to the patrol unit with several large bags and a big box of diapers.

"Wow, Sergeant Jackson must have needed quite a few things, but I didn't realize he had a baby at home, too."

"Yeah, he did need quite a few things, but the diapers are mine. Nothing like taking care of a little personal business on city time."

"Glad to hear you're good with doing personal business when we're on shift, Alex. At Baytown, there were all kinds of rules about not mixing personal with business and we were *never* allowed to use any city vehicle for anything other than city business."

"We have some of the same policies at Wills Ford, but no one really pays any attention to them. In fact, the Chief uses all kinds of department property for himself. Sarge told me the Chief has two of our new assault rifles in the gun safe at his house. This is in addition to the city-owned shot guns and handheld weapons he has at home. The way I see it, if the Chief can do it, we can, too."

"This is good information to know, Alex."

At roll call the next morning, Alexis sees Alex talking to Sergeant Jackson and notices Alex hands the Sergeant a credit card. She asks Alex about it as they are walking to their patrol unit.

"What's with you letting Sarge use your credit card? I'd think being a 15-year veteran and a sergeant he'd be loaning you his credit card!"

Whispering, Alex says, "Quiet down, Alexis. Anyone can hear you out here. We'll talk in the car."

"All right, Alex, spill."

"What you saw and what I'm going to tell you don't go beyond this car. Got it?"

"Sure, Alex. I'm your partner and you should know I have your back."

"Good to hear it. What you saw was me giving Sarge his city P-card, which he gave me yesterday to pay for the things I got him at Target."

"Oh, somehow I got the impression you were running a personal errand for him yesterday."

"I was Alexis. Don't you get it? I used his P-card for his personal stuff because he does it all the time. He even told me to throw in a box of diapers. When I was on C shift, I'd run errands for him all the time. After Zach was born, every time I went to Target for him or department business he told me to throw in a box of diapers compliments of the city. Several of the guys with young kids told me he did the same for them when their kids were in diapers."

"Good to know, I guess. At least it shows he cares about his officers. On another note, Alex, I hate to keep comparing Baytown to Wills Ford, but we had all kinds of rules about the P-cards. If something like Sarge is doing was going on in Baytown, no one ever talked about it if it was."

"Alexis, we probably have some of the same rules here in Wills Ford but it's like the no personal business on city time rules. No one pays any attention to them. According to Sarge, using P-cards for personal things is the norm, at least in our department."

"Well, I need a new microwave. Do you think Sarge would let me use his P-card for one? Just kidding, Alex. I wouldn't dream of taking diapers away from Zach!"

A few weeks later at the station, the following conversation occurs between Sergeant Templeton and his immediate supervisor, Lieutenant Joanna Mason.

"Sergeant Templeton, I told you last week we don't have money in the budget to buy a new refrigerator for the breakroom. We are only two months away from the new budget year and a new refrigerator is in the Chief's budget request."

"Look, Lieutenant. We can't wait for the new budget year. The refrigerator is on its last leg now and barely keeps our soft drinks cool much less cold. It's the middle of summer and keeping drinks cold is a priority."

"I understand, Sergeant, but we still have no budget money to replace the old one. Besides, it's only those of us who work here at the station who really use it. If you want cold soft drinks, then buy one out of the machine sitting right next to the refrigerator."

"It's your funeral when all the guys revolt."

Sergeant Templeton mutters to himself as he returns to his office.

"I'll show her who the boss really is around here. She stole my promotion last year and who says I need to listen to her anyway. I'll head to Home Depot on my way home and buy one on my P-card and she'll never know."

"Hey Captain Costello. How are you holding up since the big D was final?"

"Can't complain, Sergeant, but I do miss seeing my kids every night. It sure sounded like you were complaining about something a few minutes ago. I could hear you muttering all the way down the hall."

"It's nothing a little P-card magic can't fix. We need a new 'fridge in the breakroom and tightwad Mason won't approve it. It's the hottest part of the year and the old one is going to die any day now. Figured I'd pull an end run and get one at Home Depot tonight and put it on my P-card. Besides, she leaves tomorrow for a two-week cruise and won't see the new one until she gets back."

"Sounds like a fine plan to me, Sergeant. If she is one of those who actually looks at P-card receipts, I'll cover for you. She does need to be reminded about the chain of command every week or two. To make it look legit, why don't you get the lumber and stuff we'll need next month at the safety fair while you're there. Maybe she won't look at the receipt details. I know I never do."

"Thanks, Captain. I appreciate it."

Two weeks later Lieutenant Mason returns from her cruise and finds she has a lot of paperwork needing her attention. The paperwork includes reviewing P-card statements and receipts.

Looking at her watch, she says:

"I can't believe it's already noon. I'm not even half way through this pile and at this rate I'll get home around midnight tonight. Why did I ever think a two-week cruise was a good idea?"

At 5pm Chief Drew Peterson, walks by Lieutenant Mason's office on his way to get an early dinner before the city council meeting at 7pm.

"Welcome back, Lieutenant. I realize you are swamped but I wanted to remind you the P-card statements are due in accounting first thing in the morning. Apparently, your vacation is the reason they can't pay the bill on time this month."

"Copy that, Chief. Enjoy the council meeting tonight."

At 7pm, Lieutenant Mason is tired and ready to go home. Instead of looking at the receipts attached to the sergeant's P-card statements, to save time she simply scans the vendors on the statements and approves the statements for payment.

The following morning Lieutenant Mason walks in the breakroom and sees Sergeant Templeton talking to some patrol officers, two shift corporals, and Captain Costello. When she turns toward the coffee pot she sees the new refrigerator.

"Sergeant Templeton, would you happen to know how we got what looks to be this new refrigerator?"

"You must have been a detective once, Lieutenant, because your powers of observation are amazing."

"Cut to the chase, Sergeant. How did we get this new refrigerator?"

"Hang on, Lieutenant. Sergeant Templeton explained the situation to me and I agreed with him. I told him to buy it because we needed a new refrigerator to make it through the last two months of summer."

"Captain Costello, I appreciate you looking out for everyone, but we don't have budget money for a new refrigerator, which is why I denied Sergeant Templeton's request for a new one. How are we supposed to cover this? We are at the end of the fiscal year and none of us has any funds to transfer to cover this purchase."

"Not to worry, Lieutenant. Sergeant Templeton bought it using his P-card at the same time he bought the supplies we need for the safety fair next month. No one in accounting will ever notice we bought a new refrigerator."

"Good thinking, guys. You're right about accounting not noticing it, Captain."

The following conversation occurs six months later between Chief Drew Peterson and Captain Costello while they are playing golf.

"How's your love life, Pete? Are you getting back in the saddle again now that your divorce has been final for more than a year?"

"Can't complain, Drew. The online dating services I'm using provide me with more women than I can date at one time. Did I ever tell you I put two of the services on my P-card?"

"You know I never review your P-card activity and if you told me what you were doing I must have forgotten. Have you been doing this since your divorce or is this something new?"

"I tried it with one service a few months after the divorce because I was short of cash what with legal fees, alimony, and child support. You obviously never found it and accounting hasn't found out yet. I figure if they ever do find it I'll tell them I must have used my P-card thinking it was my credit card."

"Nice drive, Pete. You know the wife and I go to dinner at least twice a month compliments of the city. We make sure to go someplace away from the city in case someone here questions using a city card when I'm out with my wife. I used my P-card to order her flowers for her birthday last year, too. You should try it with these sweet young things you're meeting online. What female doesn't get all gooey inside when she gets flowers from her special guy?"

"Great idea to save for when I actually meet someone I really like. Let's wrap up this round and head to the 19th hole.

Four months later the city hires a new CFO and is lucky enough to find a highly qualified individual to fill the position. Two months after starting with the city the CFO, Max Rider, starts an in-depth review of the city's P-card procedures.

When Max learns oversight of P-card transactions is lax and controls are most often circumvented or ignored, he begins an in-depth investigation of P-card charges for the prior two years. His month-long investigation reveals abuse of P-cards is occurring in all departments except for the city manager's office and the accounting department. The worst abuse of the P-card system is found in the police department. After consulting with the city manager, Max agrees to start his investigation with the police department to determine if there is fraud.

The following meeting between CFO Max Rider and Chief Peterson occurs in the chief's office.

"Thanks for agreeing to meet with me this afternoon Chief. I've been busy settling in and haven't had a chance to meet with you outside of staff meetings."

"No problem, Max. I was surprised you were willing to meet on a Friday afternoon. Don't all your city hall suits leave early on Friday?"

"I can't speak for anyone other than myself, but I don't leave city hall most days until my wife calls to remind me dinner is cold."

"Boy, am I picking up what you're putting down. What can I do for you today?"

"I've been looking at a lot of things since I came on board three months ago, but I focused on P-card procedures and transactions first. This was such a bucket of worms at my last job that we cancelled all of the P-cards and went back to recurring POs."

"Well, we really enjoy the spending flexibility the P-cards give us, which is my way of asking you not to cancel all of them."

"Chief, I have a summary here of all transactions involving P-cards issued to you and your department and I'm hoping you can help me understand a few things."

"I can try, Max, but if I don't know the answers you'll have to talk to the card holder themselves."

"Not a problem, Chief, we'll start with your card and the cards for Captain Costello and Lieutenant Mason since you approve them."

"Sounds fair. What can I tell you?"

"Here's a copy of my summary to help you follow my questions. You seem to have a lot of charges for meals. By any chance do you have a log of who you took to dinner and what you discussed? The IRS kind of likes it when we have documentation of time, place, and business purpose when it comes to meals."

"No one ever told me to keep track of this information so I'm not sure if I can remember."

"Maybe I can jog your memory. Twice a month you have dinner on Friday night at an out-of-town restaurant. None of your statements have the actual receipt attached, which means I don't know what you had for dinner. Most times only the charge receipt is attached. These are time stamped and most nights you don't sign the check until after 10pm. Are you sure you can't remember anything about who you might take to dinner twice a month?"

Hearing nothing from the Chief, Max continues discussing items on the summary.

"How about these here? You have charges at the same florist every couple of months, but no receipts are ever attached to the related statement. I called the florist to see if I could get the name of the recipient and she was very helpful. Do you have a wife or daughter named 'Delores Peterson,' Chief?"

"Here are a few confusing charges at Home Depot. I say confusing because all of these transactions occurred on a Saturday or Sunday. There are several transactions over two weekends this past spring totaling over $1,500. Interestingly enough, no receipts are attached for any of these purchases as well. Can you think of what they might have been, Chief?"

"You know, Max, I don't like the way this meeting is going. I think you should leave now."

"The city manager said you might react this way but if you did, I should keep on going over things with you. How about switching our focus to Captain Costello's card charges? Can you help me understand why the city is paying for the Captain's online dating services? It seems his P-card has been charged for one service for two years and another for 18 months."

"You're going to have to ask Captain Costello about this. I must not have understood what the vendor was when I approved his statements."

"I might be able to believe you, Chief, if the line item on the statement every month didn't say 'online dating service' after the vendor's name. How about this $2,300 charge at Bed Bath & Beyond two years ago? Isn't this around the time the Captain's divorce was finalized?"

"Again, Max, I don't like the way this meeting is going, and you will need to ask Captain Costello about these things."

"Fine, Chief. I'm almost done for today, but I need to go over Lieutenant Mason's charges before I can leave."

"Make it quick, Max."

"Here's a $500 charge about a year ago to a cruise line. The cruise line actually talked to me about the charge and told me it was a deposit on a two-week cruise booked in the name of Joanna Mason. Here's another charge and I have to admit at least there is a receipt and an explanation."

"Well then, why are we talking about it?"

"It's an interesting vendor and explanation. The vendor is a well-known women's lingerie shop, which appears a bit suspicious. However, I'm willing to listen to what Lieutenant Mason might have to say about it. She wrote on the receipt the items were supplies for situational escape training. I'm not sure what this type of training is. Can you explain it, Chief?"

"This meeting is over, Max. Get out of my office right now."

"Sure thing, Chief. Please know this discussion is not over yet. I didn't even bring up what I found relating to the sergeants' P-cards. I think we'll ask the city manager to sit in on our next meeting."

Exercises

1. Aside from the fraud that occurred in this case, do you think the city's P-Card policies and procedures were adequate? Why or why not?

2. What are some controls you would add to the P-Card program?

3. Why did these situations go undetected for almost two years? What could the city manager or accounting function have done to prevent and detect this type of fraud?

4. What are some audit procedures that could be used to test controls and activity related to procurement cards?

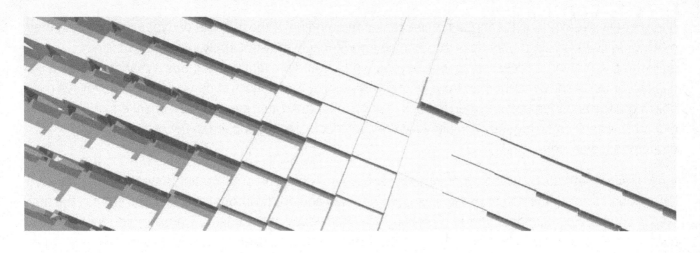

Chapter 5

Case 5: Cyber Fraud

Learning objective

- Identify various types of cyber frauds and their associated risks.

Before we start

Cyberfraud is becoming more prevalent and more costly every year and is garnering more interest in preventing it and protecting individuals and organizations from it. This is especially important for small- and medium-sized organizations because they typically have fewer controls in place than larger organizations, making them an easy target for a data breach.

According to a survey of cyber claims filed by CPA firms in 2017, 30% of all claims were due to hacking and 31% were due to human error. Social engineering and ransomware accounted for 20% and 10%, respectively, of the claims.[1]

Hackers will continue to test systems for vulnerabilities regardless of the controls an organization might put in place. Additionally, the methods hackers use change rapidly, making cyber controls in place today ineffective tomorrow. However, by implementing adequate data security measures, governmental and not-for-profit organizations may reduce the risk of a data breach or reduce the impact of a successful data breach.

---

[1] *Shore up your data breach detection skills*, Sarah Beckett, Journal of Accountancy, October 2018. Available at www.journalofaccountancy.com.

Successfully avoiding a cyber threat requires an understanding of the mindset of cybercriminals and their motivation. Synthesizing cyber risks through the fraud triangle may not apply in the cybercrime environment, making it necessary to look beyond typical fraud prevention methods. What motivates a hacker can be vastly different than from what motivates the traditional fraudster. Former employees may hold a grudge and then be motivated to hack their former employer's system. Other hackers might launch an attack on an organization because they are ideologically opposed to the organization's strategy, mission, or success.

A number of methods by which cybercriminals successfully hack an organization's system are discussed here. Understanding the nature of the data governmental and not-for-profit organizations store is the first step in establishing best practices to protecting this data. Many governments, for example, store credit card and financial institution information. Not-for-profits providing health and human services may store personal financial information as well as health and education related data.

Historically, governmental and not-for-profit organizations invest human, capital, and financial resources in front line services and mission-oriented activities rather than internal control systems. Similarly, they often make minimal or inadequate investments in technology and devote little or no resources to cybersecurity. As such, hackers find governmental and not-for-profit organizations easy targets for a cyberattack. There are, however, some controls all governmental and not-for-profit organizations, regardless of size, can implement to reduce their vulnerability to a cyberattack. These include the following:

- Train users on security practices by regularly educating employees about new attacks and risks
- Create and test system backups ensuring backups are consistent with the recovery time defined in the organization's disaster recovery plan
- Prioritize anti-virus and security patches on all systems in a timely manner
- Implement network segmentation controls that consider which individuals/functions need access to which systems and data
- Review existing insurance policies for adequacy of cyber coverage
- Create a written incident response plan to help lessen the impact of a breach should one occur
- Monitor logs from firewalls, anti-virus programs, etc.[2]

Governmental and not-for-profit organizations need to get in front of cybersecurity risks and the hackers who prey on their vulnerable systems. Best practices which can minimize vulnerability to hackers include the following:[3]

- Encrypting sensitive data and full disk encryption on all relevant equipment including mobile devices and external storage
- Using a multi-factor or two-factor authentication (known as 2FA) system for remote access
- Establishing strong controls over cloud and vendor management systems
- Performing security awareness training for all employees on a regular basis
- Including internal security controls on embedded devices such as web cameras, door badge access systems, and HVAC systems

---

[2] *Why cyberdefenses are worth the cost*. Mark Shelhart, Journal of Accountancy. November 2018.

[3] Based on the article *Inside the Mind of a Hacker: Knowing the Motivations Can Help You Mitigate the Risk of a Breach*. By Stan Sterna, JD and Nick Graf, CISSP, CEH, CIPT published in the Florida CPA Today Fall 2018 edition.

- Documenting and testing incident response plans
- Implementing a formal data retention policy, which includes processes for the secure deletion of data
- Protecting the physical security of all relevant equipment both onsite and offsite
- Conducting annual penetration tests and investigating and correcting issues identified

What is a data breach?

A *data breach* occurs when someone gains access to information that contains confidential information. This can occur because of a lack of security, the bypassing of security, or the elimination of security. Data breaches occur when information is stolen from computers and other electronic devices. Data breaches can also occur when devices containing information are lost or misplaced. Data breaches usually fall under one of the following types:

- Outsiders
- Insiders
- Accidental loss
- State sponsored

Data breaches not only inconvenience the victim companies and individuals whose information has been compromised, but they also place a significant cost on the victim. Because an organization is considered to be negligent in its duties to safeguard the information provided to it by employees, donors, customers, and others, there is a significant cost to being a victim of a data breach.

Cyber frauds

Cyber fraud and *cybercrime* are terms used to identify illegal activities involving the Internet and the use of computers or other electronic devices. Cybercrime is one of the greatest threats facing our country and has enormous implications for our national security, economic prosperity, and public safety. The range of threats and the challenges they present for law enforcement expand just as rapidly as technology evolves. Victims of cyber frauds include individuals, businesses, not-for-profits, and government entities.

Cybercrime is evolving and becoming more sophisticated. Cybercriminals now have their own social networks and even have escrow services to protect their interests when conducting transactions with other criminals. Malware can be licensed by criminals, and, if they experience issues, there are tech support teams to assist them with their crimes. Criminals can even rent botnets by the hour for their crime sprees. There is also pay-for-play malware available and an open market for zero-day exploits.[4]

---

[4] See www.knowbe4.com.

Phishing

Phishing is a cybercrime in which the criminals contact the victim through email messages that appear to come from legitimate business or government sources. Often, the email headers are spoofed to make them look legitimate. The purpose of the phishing email is to obtain information such as names, addresses, Social Security numbers, phone numbers, dates of birth, credit card numbers, and other personal information from the victims. When the victims supply the information, the criminals are able to use the information to steal the victim's identity and assets. The following are examples of various types of phishing emails.

▲ **Date: Today**		
	E-ZPass Support	Indebtedness for driving on toll road #00839442
▲ **Date: Yesterday**		
	E-ZPass Manager	Payment for driving on toll road, invoice #00162217
	District Court	Notice to Appear
	FedEx Ground	Unable to deliver your item, #000169181
▲ **Date: Last Week**		
	FedEx 2Day	Unable to deliver your item, #00000496032
	Boris Attorneys	Inheritance
	County Court	Notice to appear in Court #000933926
	State Court	Notice of appearance in Court #0000493961
	Learn Medical Bil...	High demand and good pay in medical billing careers
	FedEx 2Day A.M.	We could not deliver your parcel, #00269544
	FedEx 2Day	Courier was unable to deliver the parcel, ID000557896
	m.sourd@mdef5...	Re: 700WFQG
	FedEx Internatio...	Unable to deliver your item, #0000374620
	no-reply@discov...	Reminder: $25,000 Discover Personal Loans Video Contest
	E-ZPass Agent	Indebtedness for driving on toll road #00678129
	E-ZPass Support	Pay for driving on toll road, invoice #00000371690
	FedEx Internatio...	We could not deliver your parcel, #000729678
	Cash At Home	Local mom makes over $8740 / month!
	Technical Support	Webmail Users Maintenance Notice
▲ **Date: Two Weeks Ago**		
	Service Monitor	Alert - Information in your credit report has changed
	Passport Renewal	Renew Passport if applicable #12291217

Email example

Denial of service attacks

Denial of service attacks (DoS) occur when criminals use botnets or networks of infected computers to bring down a website or computer system by overloading its capabilities, thus, causing it to crash. In many instances, the criminals follow up on the DoS attack with an attempt to hack the system and upload malware onto the computer while the victim is busy trying to fix the problem.

The most common and obvious type of DoS attack occurs when an attacker "floods" a network with information. When you type a URL for a particular website into your browser, you are sending a request to that site's computer server to view the page. The server can only process a certain number of requests at once, so if an attacker overloads the server with requests, it can't process your request. This is a "denial of service" because you can't access that site. In a distributed denial of service (DDoS) attack, an attacker may use your computer to attack another computer. By taking advantage of security vulnerabilities or weaknesses, an attacker could take control of your computer. He or she could then force your computer to send huge amounts of data to a website or send spam to particular email addresses. The attack is "distributed" because the attacker is using multiple computers, including yours, to launch the DoS attack.[5]

Brand hacking

This cybercrime occurs when criminals post false or misleading (fraudulent) information on the Internet about a company's products or services or about the company itself. This is usually done via social media websites or blogs. The usual purpose of brand hacking is to tarnish or damage the reputation of

---

[5] Department of Homeland Security, www.us-cert.gov/ncas/tips/ST04-015.

the brand being hacked. Negative ratings on the Internet can steer customers away. A twist on the concept of brand hacking occurred when a hotel chain paid its employees to rate their "roach motel" as a four-star resort on various travel sites, enticing customers with fictitious reviews to get them to stay there.

Pharming

Pharming occurs when a virus or other malicious software is placed on the victim's computer. The malware hijacks the victim's web browser. When the victim types in the website for a legitimate company, usually a bank or financial institution, the malware directs the victim's browser to a fictitious copy of the website set up by the criminal. The criminal is hoping to capture the victim's user ID and password or other useful information. Pharming can also be done by exploiting vulnerabilities on a company's website that allows the criminals to redirect legitimate customers to a spoofed website.

Spoofing

Spoofing is a term used to describe activity that makes a fraudulent website or email look legitimate. The purpose of spoofing is to make the victim believe they are communicating with someone they know, when, in fact, they are providing information to the criminals. It is also common for criminals to spoof phone calls and text messages. The latest FBI data draws on fraud reports submitted by victims around the world from October 2013 to May 2018. In that time frame, the FBI counts 41,058 total U.S. victims who collectively lost at least $2.9 billion.

From October 2013 to May 2018, CEO email fraud collectively cost U.S. businesses at least $2.9 billion.[6] The typical CEO email spoof occurs when criminals send an email to an accounting clerk, bookkeeper, or payables manager that appears to have originated from the CEO of the company. There is usually an invoice attached with instructions to wire or ACH the funds to the vendor as soon as possible. The bank account receiving the funds is usually overseas, or, if it is in the United States, the funds are immediately transferred overseas when they are deposited. Another version of this cybercrime requires the request for copies of payroll records or W-2 and other tax records, giving the criminals access to personal information of the company's employees.

The following illustrates an example of a spoofing email.

---

[6] FBI: Global Business Email Compromise Losses Hit $12.5 Billion. https://www.bankinfosecurity.com/fbi-alert-reported-ceo-fraud-losses-hit-125-billion-a-11206 (retrieved February 28, 2019)

Spoofing example from www.knowbe4.com

Urgent Request ▢ | Inbox x | 🖨 ⬚

Stu Sjouwerman <stus@knowbe4.   7:50 AM (1 hour ago) ☆ | ↩ | ▾

to me ▾

Alanna

I want you to send me the list of W-2 copy of employees wage and tax statement for 2015, I need them in PDF file type, you can send it as an attachment. Kindly prepare the lists and email them to me asap.

⬚⬚⬚

Knowledge check

1. Phishing is usually conducted with

    a. A cell phone.
    b. An email.
    c. A rod and reel.
    d. A botnet.

Ransomware

Ransomware is a type of malware that is placed on a computer and encrypts all the files on the computer. The criminals then require that the victim pay a ransom in order to obtain the decryption key and gain access to their files again. Well-known examples of ransomware include CryptoLocker and Cryptowall 4.0. Cryptowall 4.0 is the latest version of ransomware being used by many cybercriminals to infect and encrypt all important/ most popular files (such as .xls, .wpd, .ppt, .jpg) on affected computers. Encryption is strong and is impossible to decrypt without paying the ransom (98% of attacks ask for payment to be made in Bitcoin).[7] The FBI estimates that ransomware is a $1 billion a year fraud. The following image illustrates a message that is generated once ransomware has been placed on a computer.

---

[7] See www.thenextweb.com, *Cryptocurrency ransomware payments up 90%, thanks to Ryuk.* Accessed November 6, 2019.

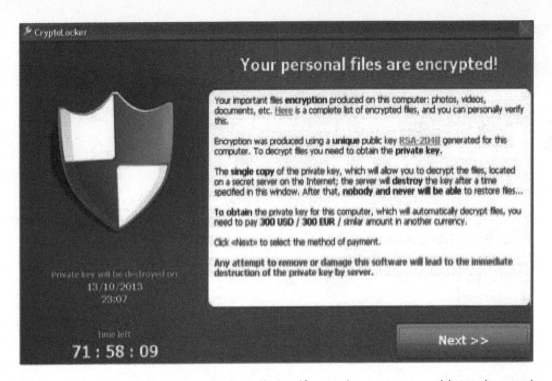

Another type of ransomware, called Reveton, installs itself onto the computer without the user's knowledge. Then, the computer freezes and a bogus message from the FBI pops up on the screen saying the user violated federal law, as shown in the following image. To unlock the computer, the user must pay a fine.[8]

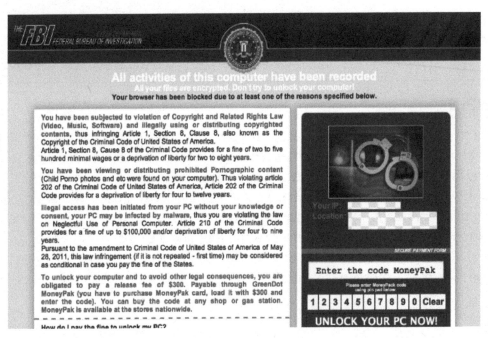

For a single computer, the cybercriminals will initially request a smaller ransom and demand larger ransoms when more computers are infected with the ransomware. Once the deadline for the payment

---

[8] See www.fbi.gov/audio-repository/news-podcasts-thisweek-reveton-ransomware/*view*.

has passed, the criminals increase the ransom demand.[9] According to a cybersecurity company, Coveware, in the first quarter of 2019 organizations paid an average ransom of $12,762 per incident. This is almost double the average amount of $6,733 paid in the fourth quarter of 2018.[10]

Typical ransomware software uses RSA 2048 encryption to encrypt files. Just to give you an idea of how strong this is, an average desktop computer is estimated to take around 6.4 quadrillion years to crack an RSA 2048 key.[11]

On August 9, 2016, the FBI changed its position on paying the Bitcoin ransom to the cyber criminals. Supervisory special agent for the FBI's Cyber Division, Will Bales, said that businesses or individuals targeted by ransomware should refuse to pay the ransom. The U.S. Department of Justice stated there are approximately 4,000 ransomware attacks daily in the United States.

On September 27, 2016, the governor of California signed Senate Bill 1137, making ransomware a form of extortion, even if the victim does not pay the ransom.

Section 523 of the Penal Code[12] is amended to read:

Chapter 523.

(a) Every person who, with intent to extort any money or other property from another, sends or delivers to any person any letter or other writing, whether subscribed or not, expressing or implying, or adapted to imply, any threat such as is specified in Section 519 is punishable in the same manner as if such money or property were actually obtained by means of such threat.

(b) (1) Every person who, with intent to extort money or other consideration from another, introduces ransomware into any computer, computer system, or computer network is punishable pursuant to Section 520 in the same manner as if such money or other consideration were actually obtained by means of the ransomware.

(2) Prosecution pursuant to this subdivision does not prohibit or limit prosecution under any other law.

(c) (1) "Ransomware" means a computer contaminant, as defined in Section 502, or lock placed or introduced without authorization into a computer, computer system, or computer network that restricts access by an authorized person to the computer, computer system, computer network, or any data therein under circumstances in which the person responsible for the placement or introduction of the ransomware demands payment of money or other consideration to remove the computer contaminant, restore access to the computer, computer system, computer network, or data, or otherwise remediate the impact of the computer contaminant or lock.

(2) A person is responsible for placing or introducing ransomware into a computer, computer system, or computer network if the person directly places or introduces the ransomware or directs or induces another person to do so, with the intent of demanding payment or other consideration to remove the ransomware, restore access, or otherwise remediate the impact of the ransomware.

---

[9] See footnote 4.

[10] See www.zdnet.com, *Ransomware: The cost of rescuing your files is going up as attackers get more sophisticated*, by Danny Palmer. April 16, 2019.

[11] See footnote 4.

[12] See leginfo.legislature.ca.gov/faces/billCompareClient.xhtml?bill_id=201520160SB1137.

Hacking

Hacking is commonly executed by placing malware on a computer system in order to allow the criminals to gain control of the computer or to gain access to information stored on the computer. Currently, computers, cell phones, and other electronic devices are the main target of cybercriminals. As the world is becoming more automated, cybercriminals are increasingly attacking robots and automated production systems in addition to information systems.

A common tool used by cybercriminals is a computer virus. A *virus* is a segment of computer code that attaches itself to a program, such as Microsoft Office, that is already loaded on the computer. A computer virus can cause the infected program to delete, email, or copy files or perform other actions. A computer virus creates copies of itself that it inserts in data files and uninfected programs.

Another common type of malware is known as a *Trojan horse* or *Trojan*. A Trojan is a malware program that is disguised as something else, usually a program or application that the user wanted. Trojans, unlike viruses, are stand-alone programs and do not need to infect a program already installed on the computer. Trojans are often used to load spyware onto infected computers or make them part of a botnet. Trojans often infect computers by piggy-backing on a free program or application downloaded by the user of the device.

A *computer worm* is a type of malware that transmits itself over networks and the Internet and infects any computer connecting with an infected source. Computer worms can be transferred by linking to infected websites. A computer worm is like a Trojan in that it is a stand-alone program that does not need to attach itself to an existing program on the computer. A computer worm can carry a payload such as a ransomware program. The most common payload is a program that installs a backdoor on the infected computer.

Rootkits are another type of malware. A *rootkit* is specifically designed to modify the operating system of an infected computer. The main purpose of a rootkit program is to hide other malware from the user. Because a rootkit program has administrator access, it is not only able to modify the operating system but can also modify any other software installed on the computer. It is difficult to detect rootkits because the rootkit can subvert the software being used to detect the rootkit.

A very dangerous type of malware is known as a *backdoor*. A backdoor allows the cybercriminal unimpeded access to the infected computer, allowing the criminal to bypass the normal authentication processes. A backdoor usually provides the hacker with administrative access to the infected computer.

Mobile malware

Another method for infecting devices is through a charging station. Cybercriminals load malware onto charging stations located in public places like airports, malls, sports arenas, and subways. Unsuspecting users use their USB ports to connect to the charging stations to recharge batteries in their devices. While they are connected, the data on their devices are copied, and malware is installed.

Malvertising

Criminals convince ad networks that they are legitimate businesses. The criminals then place ads containing malware on the networks or they link to sites containing malware. The criminals attach malware to ads that appear on legitimate websites so that when the ads are opened the malware is placed on the victim's computer.[13]

Spyware

Spyware is software that tries to gather information about a person or organization without their knowledge or consent and then may send the information to another entity. Spyware may also take control of a computer without the user's knowledge. Some popular versions of spyware for cell phones are as follows:

- HighsterMobile
- Spyera
- Spyrix
- FlexiSpy
- Mobile Spy
- MobiStealth
- mSpy

Popular versions of other types of spyware include the following:

- Keylogger
- Win-Spy
- Spytech Spy Agent
- SpectorSoft
- 007 Spy Software

Knowledge check

2. Which type of malware attacks an application program that is already installed on the victim's computer?

    a. Rootkit.
    b. Backdoor.
    c. Trojan horse.
    d. Virus.

---

[13] See footnote 4.

Background

Oceanside was incorporated over 300 years ago and in the last 30 years has grown from a small sleepy village to a bustling beach vacation destination with a vibrant arts community. As the city grew, the increase in tourism provided the city with significant financial resources to invest in human and capital resources. However, over the last five years, it has been challenging for the city's information technology staff to keep up with the ever-increasing pace of technological advances and the proliferation of social media in the business environment.

The city's information technology (IT) department consists of a director and two technology specialists, all of which possess the skills, knowledge, and experience to perform their jobs effectively. Staffing has been considered adequate in the past as the city purchases off-the-shelf software for all applications and contracts with outside specialists if any modifications are needed. Additionally, the finance director and assistant finance director also possess an adequate knowledge of information technology and its role in the city's operations.

Responsibilities of the IT department include the following:

- Administration of the city's intranet and external email functions
- Monitoring employee access to the Internet for appropriateness and applicability to city operations
- Troubleshooting user issues with application software
- Maintenance of IT equipment and hardware (including the city's various servers and cloud-based operations)

The case

The following conversation takes place after the weekly meeting of all department heads with the city manager between CFO Anaba Sandoval and IT Director Faisal Shirani.

"Hey Faisal, I'm going to the AICPA's Government Conference next week and I was trying to decide what sessions to attend and I noticed there are a lot of sessions relating to cybersecurity. What type of topics should I be looking for when deciding which of these sessions to attend?"

"Well, Anaba, as you know cybersecurity is a hot topic these days and means something different to almost everyone. As an IT guy, I probably look at cybersecurity differently than you would, being focused on accounting and such."

"I guess you're right and I know we've had a few discussions in the last year about where my financial management system may be susceptible to a cyberattack but surely you have something to recommend. Faisal, if you have some time now could you walk with me to my office and I can show you the cybersecurity sessions the conference offers?"

"Sure, Anaba, I can look at things and make some suggestions."

The next week at the AICPA Government Conference, Anaba sees a friend of hers, Abigail Wester, who is the CFO for a large mid-western city.

"Hey there, Abigail. Imagine running into you at this conference. There must be 1,800 people here and I run into you the first day of the conference."

"You know what they say, Anaba, it is truly a small world. How have you been? It seems as if we haven't seen each other in ages."

"Things are good on the home front as well as at work. Oceanside is still growing, and we are still lucky enough to have significant revenues to cover the cost of our services. How about things with you?"

"Well, the rust belt isn't as lucky as you folks on the coast and we are still facing revenue shortfalls even though the Great Recession has been over for a long time. I'd give anything to be able to fund current services instead of having to look at cutting them every year."

"I know we are lucky Abigail and I'd not want to be in your shoes. Oh no, it's time for my next session."

"Where are you heading, Anaba?"

"Well, at the suggestion of my IT director, I'm sitting in on cybersecurity orientation session. Faisal said it would be good for me to sit in on an overview session before any of the more technical sessions."

"Well girlfriend, great minds think alike because I'm heading to the same session for the same reason! Let's get moving."

Twenty minutes into the cybersecurity orientation session, Anaba abruptly leaves the session and doesn't return. During the next break, Abigail seeks out Anaba and finds her in the cyber café talking animatedly on her phone. After seeing how agitated Anaba is, Abigail can't help but listen to the conversation.

"Listen Faisal, I didn't send an email to the city manager asking him to execute a $30,000 wire transfer. I'm telling you like I told Jim, I would never ask him to approve a wire transfer of any amount without discussing it with him in person first."

"Thank goodness Jim contacted me to verify the instructions in the message before he took any action. As soon as I saw the message from him I immediately left my session. Ironically, I was in the cybersecurity overview session you recommended."

"Yes, the message wasn't really written in my style even though it referenced a vendor on our approved vendor list. What I feel like an idiot about is neither Jim nor I noticed his last name was misspelled. I guess when your brain expects to see 'Martin,' it doesn't see 'Marten.'"

"I know, I couldn't believe it either. Who knew Jim would notice the request was to pay a construction contractor for consulting services? I guess his certified transportation planner status is good for more than planning road projects!"

"All right. I'll see you when I get back in the office on Thursday."

Anaba disconnects from the call and sees Abigail sitting at the station next to her.

"OK. Spill it Anaba. What is the world is going on with you? I shamelessly listened to your end of the conversation and it sounds like you had some kind of cyber incident."

"Abigail, it was something right out of our session this morning or at least the part of the session I managed to attend."

"Give me the deets and don't leave out anything!"

"Well, you know I left the session soon after it started, and it was because I got a strange email from our city manager. He was asking me why we were paying $30,000 to a construction contractor for consulting services. I had no idea what he was talking about and I left the session to call him."

"Ooh, this sounds like the spoofing thing they discussed in the session after you left."

"Spoofing or loofing, it is scary what happened. The city manager received an email from me from what looked exactly like my city email account but didn't think the wording in it sounded like me. The bank the wire was to be sent to is actually a large regional community bank in our area and the vendor was one we have used before. Jim didn't notice it, but our IT director figured out the spelling of the vendor name in the email was a letter off from the way it is spelled in our approved vendor list — one 'm' instead of two. We are very fortunate the city manager noticed the vendor was a construction company and wondered why we would be paying them for consulting services."

"Wow, Anaba, it sounds like you guys dodged a bullet today. I guess this means you'll be attending all of the remaining cybersecurity sessions!"

"You've got that right, Abigail. I've known cybersecurity was important but having something happen in your own back yard elevates everything to DEFCON 1."

Exercises

1. What type of cyber fraud is represented in this case?

2. Have you or anyone you know been the victim of this type of cyber fraud? If so, what were the factors contributing to the breach? Was the fraud successful? What procedures and/or controls were implemented as a result of the breach?

3. What is your major cyber fraud concern? What are you and your organization doing to addressing cybersecurity concerns?

Exempt Organizations Glossary

Governmental terminology

accounting system. The methods and records established to identify, assemble, analyze, classify, record, and report a government's transactions and to maintain accountability for the related assets and liabilities.

accrual basis of accounting. The recording of financial effects on a government of transactions and other events and circumstances that have consequences for the government in the periods in which those transactions, events, and circumstances occur, rather than only in the periods in which cash is received or paid by the government.

ad valorem tax. A tax based on value (such as a property tax).

advance from other funds. An asset account used to record noncurrent portions of a long-term debt owed by one fund to another fund within the same reporting entity. (See **due to other funds** and **interfund receivable/payable**).

appropriation. A legal authorization granted by a legislative body to make expenditures and to incur obligations for specific purposes. An appropriation is usually limited in the amount and time it may be expended.

assigned fund balance. A portion of fund balance that includes amounts that are constrained by the government's intent to be used for specific purposes, but that are neither restricted nor committed.

basis of accounting. A term used to refer to *when* revenues, expenditures, expenses, and transfers, and related assets and liabilities are recognized in the accounts and reported in the financial statements. Specifically, it relates to the timing of the measurements made, regardless of the nature of the measurement. (See **accrual basis of accounting**, **cash basis of accounting**, and **modified accrual basis of accounting**).

bond. A written promise to pay a specified sum of money (the face value or principal amount) at a specified date or dates in the future (the maturity dates[s]), together with periodic interest at a specified rate. Sometimes, however, all or a substantial part of the interest is included in the face value of the security. The difference between a note and bond is that the latter is issued for a longer period and requires greater legal formality.

business type activities. Those activities of a government carried out primarily to provide specific services in exchange for a specific user charge.

capital grants. Grants restricted by the grantor for the acquisition or construction, or both, of capital assets.

capital projects fund. A fund used to account for and report financial resources that are restricted, committed, or assigned to expenditures for capital outlays, including the acquisition or construction of capital facilities and other capital assets. Capital project funds exclude those types of capital-related outflows financed by proprietary funds or for assets that will be held in trust for individuals, private organizations, or other governments.

cash basis of accounting. A basis of accounting that requires the recognition of transactions only when cash is received or disbursed.

committed fund balance. A portion of fund balance that includes amounts that can only be used for specific purposes pursuant to constraints imposed by formal action of the government's highest level of decision-making authority.

consumption method. The method of accounting that requires the recognition of an expenditure or expense as inventories are used.

contributed capital. Contributed capital is created when a general capital asset is transferred to a proprietary fund or when a grant is received that is externally restricted to capital acquisition or construction. Contributions restricted to capital acquisition and construction and capital assets received from developers are reported in the operating statement as a separate item after nonoperating revenues and expenses.

custodial fund. A fiduciary fund used to account for financial resources not administered through a trust or equivalent arrangement meeting specified criteria, and that are not required to be reported in a pension (and other employee benefit) trust fund, investment trust fund, or private-purpose trust fund.

debt service fund. A fund used to account for and report financial resources that are restricted, committed, or assigned to expenditure for principal and interest. Debt service funds should be used to report resources if legally mandated. Financial resources that are being accumulated for principal and interest maturing in future years should also be reported as debt service funds.

deferred inflow of resources. An acquisition of net assets by a government that is applicable to a future reporting period.

deferred outflow of resources. A consumption of net asset by a government that is applicable to a future reporting period.

deficit. (*a*) The excess of the liabilities of a fund over its assets. (*b*) The excess of expenditures over revenues during an accounting period or, in the case of proprietary funds, the excess of expenses over revenues during an accounting period.

disbursement. A payment made in cash or by check. Expenses are only recognized at the time physical cash is disbursed.

due from other funds. A current asset account used to indicate an account reflecting amounts owed to a particular fund by another fund for goods sold or services rendered. This account includes only short-term obligations on an open account, not interfund loans.

---

due to other funds. A current liability account reflecting amounts owed by a particular fund to another fund for goods sold or services rendered. This account includes only short-term obligations on an open account, not interfund loans.

enabling legislation. Legislation that authorizes a government to assess, levy, charge, or otherwise mandate payment of resources from external resource providers and includes a legally enforceable requirement that those resources be used for the specific purposes stipulated in the legislation.

encumbrances. Commitments related to unperformed (executory) contracts for goods or services. Used in budgeting, encumbrances are not generally accepted accounting principles (GAAP) expenditures or liabilities but represent the estimated amount of expenditures that will ultimately result if unperformed contracts in process are completed.

enterprise fund. A fund established to account for operations financed and operated in a manner similar to private business enterprises (such as gas, utilities, transit systems, and parking garages). Usually, the governing body intends that costs of providing goods or services to the general public be recovered primarily through user charges.

expenditures. Decreases in net financial resources. Expenditures include current operating expenses requiring the present or future use of net current assets, debt service and capital outlays, intergovernmental grants, entitlements, and shared revenues.

expenses. Outflows or other consumption of assets or incurrences of liabilities, or a combination of both, from delivering or producing goods, rendering services, or carrying out other activities that constitute the entity's ongoing major or central operations.

fiduciary fund. A fund that reports fiduciary activities meeting the criteria in paragraphs 6–11 of GASB Statement No. 84, *Fiduciary Activities*. Financial reporting is focused on reporting net position and changes in net position.

fund. A fiscal and accounting entity with a self-balancing set of accounts in which cash and other financial resources, all related liabilities and residual equities, or balances, and changes therein, are recorded and segregated to carry on specific activities or attain certain objectives in accordance with special regulations, restrictions, or limitations.

fund balance. The difference between fund assets and fund liabilities of the generic fund types within the governmental category of funds.

fund financial statements. Each fund has its own set of self-balancing accounts and fund financial statements that focus on information about the government's governmental, proprietary, and fiduciary fund types.

fund type. The 11 generic funds that all transactions of a government are recorded into. The 11 fund types are as follows: general, special revenue, debt service, capital projects, permanent, enterprise, internal service, private-purpose trust, pension (and other employee benefit) trust, investment trust, and custodial.

GASB. The Governmental Accounting Standards Board (GASB), organized in 1984 by the Financial Accounting Foundation (FAF) to establish standards of financial accounting and reporting for state and local governmental entities. Its standards guide the preparation of external financial reports of those entities.

general fund. The fund within the governmental category used to account for all financial resources, except those required to be accounted for in another governmental fund.

general-purpose governments. Governmental entities that provide a range of services, such as states, cities, counties, towns, and villages.

governmental funds. Funds used to account for the acquisition, use, and balances of spendable financial resources and the related current liabilities, except those accounted for in proprietary funds and fiduciary funds. Essentially, these funds are accounting segregations of financial resources. Spendable assets are assigned to a particular government fund type according to the purposes for which they may or must be used. Current liabilities are assigned to the fund type from which they are to be paid. The difference between the assets and liabilities of governmental fund types is referred to as *fund balance*. The measurement focus in these fund types is on the determination of financial position and changes in financial position (sources, uses, and balances of financial resources), rather than on net income determination.

government-wide financial statements. Highly aggregated financial statements that present financial information for all assets (including infrastructure capital assets), liabilities, and net assets of a primary government and its component units, except for fiduciary funds. The government-wide financial statements use the economic resources measurement focus and accrual basis of accounting.

infrastructure assets. Long-lived capital assets that normally are stationary in nature and can be preserved for a significantly greater number of years than most capital assets. Examples of infrastructure assets are roads, bridges, tunnels, drainage systems, water and sewer systems, dams, and lighting systems. Buildings, except those that are an ancillary part of a network of infrastructure assets, are not considered infrastructure assets.

interfund receivable/payable. Activity between funds of a government reflecting amounts provided with a requirement for repayment, or sales and purchases of goods and services between funds approximating their external exchange value (also referred to as **interfund loans** or **interfund services provided and used**).

internal service fund. A generic fund type within the proprietary category used to account for the financing of goods or services provided by one department or agency to other departments or agencies of a government, or to other governments, on a cost-reimbursement basis.

investment trust fund. A generic fund type within the fiduciary category used by a government in a fiduciary capacity, such as to maintain its cash and investment pool for other governments.

major funds. A government's general fund (or its equivalent), other individual governmental type, and enterprise funds that meet specific quantitative criteria, and any other governmental or enterprise fund that a government's officials believe is particularly important to financial statement users.

management's discussion and analysis. Management's discussion and analysis, or MD&A, is required supplementary information that introduces the basic financial statements by presenting certain financial information as well as management's analytical insights on that information.

measurement focus. The accounting convention that determines (*a*) which assets and which liabilities are included on a government's balance sheet and where they are reported, and (*b*) whether an operating statement presents information on the flow of financial resources (revenues and expenditures) or information on the flow of economic resources (revenues and expenses).

modified accrual basis of accounting. The basis of accounting adapted to the governmental fund type measurement focus. Revenues and other financial resource increments are recognized when they become both *measurable* and *available to finance expenditures of the current period*. *Available* means collectible in the current period or soon enough thereafter to be used to pay liabilities of the current period. Expenditures are recognized when the fund liability is incurred and expected to be paid from current resources, except for (*a*) inventories of materials and supplies that may be considered expenditures either when purchased or when used, and (*b*) prepaid insurance and similar items that may be considered expenditures either when paid for or when consumed. All governmental funds are accounted for using the modified accrual basis of accounting in fund financial statements.

modified approach. Rules that allow infrastructure assets that are part of a network or subsystem of a network not to be depreciated as long as certain requirements are met.

net position. The residual of all other elements presented in a statement of financial position.

nonspendable fund balance. The portion of fund balance that includes amounts that cannot be spent because they are either (*a*) not in spendable form or (*b*) legally or contractually required to be maintained intact.

pension (and other employee benefit) trust fund. A trust fund used to account for a public employees retirement system, OPEB plan, or other employee benefits other than pensions that are administered through trusts that meet specified criteria. Pension (and other employee benefit) trust funds use the accrual basis of accounting and the flow of economic resources measurement focus.

permanent fund. A generic fund type under the governmental category used to report resources that are legally restricted to the extent that only earnings, and not principal, may be used for purposes that support the reporting government's programs and, therefore, are for the benefit of the government or its citizenry. (Permanent funds do not include private-purpose trust funds, which should be used when the government is required to use the principal or earnings for the benefit of individuals, private organizations, or other governments).

private purpose trust fund. A general fund type under the fiduciary category used to report resources held and administered by the reporting government acting in a fiduciary capacity for individuals, other governments, or private organizations.

proprietary funds. The government category used to account for a government's ongoing organizations and activities that are similar to those often found in the private sector (these are enterprise and internal service funds). All assets, liabilities, equities, revenues, expenses, and transfers relating to the government's business and quasi-business activities are accounted for through proprietary funds. Proprietary funds should apply all applicable GASB pronouncements and those GAAP applicable to similar businesses in the private sector, unless those conflict with GASB pronouncements. These funds use the accrual basis of accounting in conjunction with the flow of economic resources measurement focus.

purchases method. The method under which inventories are recorded as expenditures when acquired.

restricted fund balance. Portion of fund balance that reflects constraints placed on the use of resources (other than nonspendable items) that are either (*a*) externally imposed by a creditor, such as through debt covenants, grantors, contributors, or laws or regulations of other governments or (*b*) imposed by law through constitutional provisions or enabling legislation.

required supplementary information. GAAP specify that certain information be presented as required supplementary information, or RSI.

special-purpose governments. Legally separate entities that perform only one activity or a few activities, such as cemetery districts, school districts, colleges and universities, utilities, hospitals and other health care organizations, and public employee retirement systems.

special revenue fund. A fund that must have revenue or proceeds from specific revenue sources that are either restricted or committed for a specific purpose other than debt service or capital projects. This definition means that in order to be considered a special revenue fund, there must be one or more revenue sources upon which reporting the activity in a separate fund is predicated.

interfund transfers. All transfers, such as legally authorized transfers from a fund receiving revenue to a fund through which the resources are to be expended, where there is no intent to repay. Interfund transfers are recorded on the operating statement.

unassigned fund balance. Residual classification for the general fund. This classification represents fund balance that has not been assigned to other funds and has not been restricted, committed, or assigned to specific purposes within the general fund. The general fund should be the only fund that reports a positive unassigned fund balance amount. In other funds, if expenditures incurred for specific purposes exceeded the amounts restricted, committed, or assigned to those purposes, it may be necessary to report a negative unassigned fund balance.

unrestricted fund balance. The total of committed fund balance, assigned fund balance, and unassigned fund balance.

Not-for-profit terminology

board-designated endowment fund. An endowment fund created by a not-for-profit entity's governing board by designating a portion of its net assets without donor restrictions to be invested to provide income for a long, but not necessarily specified, period. In rare circumstances, a board-designated endowment fund also can include a portion of net assets with donor restrictions. For example, if a not-for-profit is unable to spend donor-restricted contributions in the near term, then the board sometimes considers the long-term investment of these funds.

board-designated net assets. Net assets without donor restrictions subject to self-imposed limits by action of the governing board. Board-designated net assets may be earmarked for future programs, investment, contingencies, purchase or construction of fixed assets, or other uses. Some governing boards may delegate designation decisions to internal management. Such designations are considered to be included in board-designated net assets.

charitable lead trust. A trust established in connection with a split-interest agreement in which the not-for-profit entity receives distributions during the agreement's term. Upon termination of the trust, the remainder of the trust assets are paid to the donor or to third-party beneficiaries designated by the donor.

charitable remainder trust. A trust established in connection with a split-interest agreement in which the donor or a third-party beneficiary receives specified distributions during the agreement's term. Upon termination of the trust, a not-for-profit entity receives the assets remaining in the trust.

collections. Works of art, historical treasures, or similar assets that are (*a*) held for public exhibition, education, or research in furtherance of public service, rather than financial gain; (*b*) protected, kept unencumbered, cared for, and preserved; and (*c*) subject to an organizational policy that requires the proceeds of items that are sold to be used to acquire other items for collections.

conditional promise to give. A promise to give that is subject to a donor-imposed condition.

contribution. An unconditional transfer of cash or other assets, as well as unconditional promises to give, to an entity or a reduction, settlement, or cancellation of its liabilities in a voluntary nonreciprocal transfer by another entity acting other than as an owner.

costs of joint activities. Costs incurred for a joint activity. Costs of joint activities may include joint costs and costs other than joint costs. *Costs other than joint costs* are costs that are identifiable with a particular function, such as program, fund-raising, management and general, and membership development costs.

donor-imposed restriction. A donor stipulation (*donors* include other types of contributors, including makers of certain grants) that specifies a use for the contributed asset that is more specific than broad limits resulting from the nature of the organization, the environment in which it operates, and the purposes specified in its articles of incorporation or bylaws, or comparable documents for an unincorporated association. A restriction on an organization's use of the asset contributed may be temporary in nature or perpetual in nature.

donor-restricted endowment fund. An endowment fund that is created by a donor stipulation (*donors* include other types of contributors, including makers of certain grants) that requires investment of the gift in perpetuity or for a specified term. Some donors or laws may require that a portion of income, gains, or both be added to the gift and invested subject to similar restrictions.

donor-restricted support. Donor-restricted revenues or gains from contributions that increase net assets with donor restrictions (*donors* include other types of contributions, including makers of certain grants).

economic interest. A not-for-profit entity's interest in another entity that exists if any of the following criteria are met: (*a*) The other entity holds or uses significant resources that must be used for the purposes of the not-for-profit entity, either directly or indirectly, by producing income or providing services, or (*b*) the not-for-profit entity is responsible for the liabilities of the other entity.

endowment fund. An established fund of cash, securities, or other assets that provides income for the maintenance of a not-for-profit entity. The use of the assets of the fund may be with or without donor-imposed restrictions. Endowment funds generally are established by donor-restricted gifts and bequests to provide a source of income.

functional expense classification. A method of grouping expenses according to the purpose for which the costs are incurred. The primary functional classifications of a not-for-profit entity are program services and supporting activities.

funds functioning as endowment. Net assets without donor restrictions (*donors* include other types of contributors, including makers of certain grants) designated by an entity's governing board to be invested to provide income for generally a long, but not necessarily specified, period.

joint activity. An activity that is part of the fund-raising function and has elements of one or more other functions, such as programs, management and general, membership development, or any other functional category used by the entity.

joint costs. The costs of conducting joint activities that are not identifiable with a particular component of the activity.

management and general activities. Supporting activities that are not directly identifiable with one or more programs, fund-raising activities, or membership development activities.

natural expense classification. A method of grouping expenses according to the kinds of economic benefits received in incurring those expenses. Examples of natural expense classifications include salaries and wages, employee benefits, professional services, supplies, interest expense, rent, utilities, and depreciation.

net assets. The excess or deficiency of assets over liabilities of a not-for-profit entity, which is divided into two mutually exclusive classes according to the existence or absence of donor-imposed restrictions.

net assets with donor restrictions. The part of net assets of a not-for-profit entity that is subject to donor-imposed restrictions (*donors* include other types of contributors, including makers of certain grants).

net assets without donor restrictions. The part of net assets of a not-for-profit entity that is not subject to donor-imposed restrictions (*donors* include other types of contributors, including makers of certain grants).

programmatic investing. The activity of making loans or other investments that are directed at carrying out a not-for-profit entity's purpose for existence, rather than investing in the general production of income or appreciation of an asset (for example, total return investing). An example of programmatic investing is a loan made to lower-income individuals to promote home ownership.

promise to give. A written or oral agreement to contribute cash or other assets to another entity. A promise to give may be either conditional or unconditional.

underwater endowment fund. A donor-restricted endowment fund for which the fair value of the fund at the reporting date is less than either the original gift amount or the amount required to be maintained by the donor or by law that extends donor restrictions.

Single audit and Yellow Book terminology

attestation engagements. Attestation engagements concern examining, reviewing, or performing agreed-upon procedures on a subject matter or an assertion about a subject matter and reporting on the results.

compliance supplement. A document issued annually in the spring by the OMB to provide guidance to auditors.

data collection form. A form submitted to the Federal Audit Clearinghouse that provides information about the auditor, the auditee and its federal programs, and the results of the audit.

federal financial assistance. Assistance that nonfederal entities receive or administer in the form of grants, loans, loan guarantees, property, cooperative agreements, interest subsidies, insurance, food commodities, direct appropriations, or other assistance, but does not include amounts received as reimbursement for services rendered to individuals in accordance with guidance issued by the director.

financial audits. Financial audits are primarily concerned with providing reasonable assurance about whether financial statements are presented fairly, in all material respects, in conformity with GAAP or with a comprehensive basis of accounting other than GAAP.

GAGAS. Generally accepted government auditing standards issued by the GAO. They are published as *Government Auditing Standards*, also commonly known as the Yellow Book.

GAO. The United States Government Accountability Office. Among its responsibilities is the issuance of GAGAS.

OMB. The Office of Management and Budget. The OMB assists the President in the development and implementation of budget, program, management, and regulatory policies.

pass-through entity. A nonfederal entity that provides federal awards to a subrecipient to carry out a federal program.

performance audits. Performance audits entail an objective and systematic examination of evidence to provide an independent assessment of the performance and management of a program against objective criteria as well as assessments that provide a prospective focus or that synthesize information on best practices or cross-cutting issues.

program-specific audit. A compliance audit of one federal program.

single audit. An audit of a nonfederal entity that includes the entity's financial statements and federal awards.

single audit guide. This AICPA Audit Guide, formally titled Government Auditing Standards *and Single Audits*, is the former Statement of Position (SOP) 98-3, *Audits of States, Local Governments, and Not-for-Profit Organizations Receiving Federal Awards*. The single audit guide provides guidance on the auditor's responsibilities when conducting a single audit or program-specific audit in accordance with the Single Audit Act, GAGAS, and the Uniform Guidance.

subrecipient. A nonfederal entity that receives federal awards through another nonfederal entity to carry out a federal program but does not include an individual who receives financial assistance through such awards.

Uniform Guidance. Formally known as Title 2 U.S. *Code of Federal Regulations* Part 200, *Uniform Administrative Requirements, Cost Principles, and Audit Requirements for Federal Awards*. The Uniform Guidance sets forth the requirements for the compliance audit portion of a single audit.

Index

REAL FRAUDS FOUND IN GOVERNMENTS

BY LYNDA DENNIS, PH.D., CPA, CGFO

Solutions

The AICPA publishes *CPA Letter Daily*, a free e-newsletter published each weekday. The newsletter, which covers the 10-12 most important stories in business, finance, and accounting, as well as AICPA information, was created to deliver news to CPAs and others who work with the accounting profession. Besides summarizing media articles, commentaries, and research results, the e-newsletter links to television broadcasts and videos and features reader polls. *CPA Letter Daily*'s editors scan hundreds of publications and websites, selecting the most relevant and important news so you don't have to. The newsletter arrives in your inbox early in the morning. To sign up, visit smartbrief.com/CPA.

Do you need high-quality technical assistance? The AICPA Auditing and Accounting Technical Hotline provides non-authoritative guidance on accounting, auditing, attestation, and compilation and review standards. The hotline can be reached at 877.242.7212.

Solutions

Chapter 1

Suggested solutions to Case 1

1. By misstating the interim quarterly information, the city appeared to be in compliance with its bond covenants when in fact it was not. In this case, management override occurred when Michael used his system access to adjust the utility billing and collection records. In this case, no one appears to review transactions executed by the finance director. Even if the city manager were reviewing the adjustments made by the finance director, he may not have understood them. In this case, it is likely the city manager would have agreed with what Michael did to avoid the potential the bonds were called. It is also likely he might have further involved himself in the fraud as he felt his job was in jeopardy.

2. The following preliminary procedures might have detected this situation:

   - Review of transactions occurring outside the normal billing and collection cycle in the integrated utility system
   - Inquirie of the city manager as well as other managers (for example, public works or utilities staff) and administrative staff
   - Reviewing bond covenants for potential pressure on management (management pressure or incentive to meet the covenants)
   - Review of the controls over manually billings and customer write offs (potential for management override by the finance director)

3. Other procedures, that might have detected this situation, would include the following:

   - Review of quarterly information (including tracing amounts to reports, documentation, and so on) sent to bond oversight agencies
   - Confirmation with customers of aged amounts due (this may be efficient when done for customers with large balances or large overdue amounts)
   - Analytical review of collections by month and by type of customer (ratio collected, comparison with prior years, and the like)
   - Review of transactions occurring outside the normal billing and collection cycle

4. Based on AU-C section No. 240, *Consideration of Fraud in a Financial Statement Audit* (AICPA *Professional Standards*), if the auditor has identified a fraud or has obtained information that indicates that a fraud may exist, the auditor should communicate these matters on a timely basis to the appropriate level of management in order to inform those with primary responsibility for the prevention and detection of fraud of matters relevant to their

responsibilities. In this case, the auditor would communicate this situation to both the city manager and those charged with governance (for example, the city council or city audit committee) as it was perpetrated by management (the finance director). Additionally, if the auditor identifies or suspects a fraud, the auditor should determine whether the auditor has a responsibility to report the occurrence or suspicion to a party outside the entity. Although the auditor's professional duty to maintain the confidentiality of client information may preclude such reporting, the auditor's legal responsibilities may override the duty of confidentiality in some circumstances.

Knowledge check solutions

1.
   a. Incorrect. Billing schemes are an area where management may override existing controls.
   b. Incorrect. Journal entries are an area where management may override existing controls.
   c. Incorrect. Estimates are an area where management may override existing controls.
   d. Correct. Price fixing between two vendors is not something an entity controls; therefore, management cannot override any of the entity's controls in this circumstance.

2.
   a. Correct. Jackson City is a full service, medium-sized county.
   b. Incorrect. The city has grown rapidly over the last 40 years.
   c. Incorrect. The city is one of the larger cities in the state.
   d. Incorrect. Jackson City issued bonds to fund construction of a nuclear power plant.

3.
   a. Incorrect. The city and the trustee for the bonds entered into a number of covenants with respect to the utility revenue bonds.
   b. Correct. Should any of the covenants related to the utility revenue bonds be violated, the bonds may be called by the trustee.
   c. Incorrect. The city is required to have audited financial statements.
   d. Incorrect. The finance director manipulated utility billing and collection records in the current year to meet bond covenants.

Chapter 2

Suggested solutions to Case 2

1. Purchases need to be reviewed by persons having the technical knowledge to determine the propriety and reasonableness of the purchase. In addition, management can develop financial and operational expectations and then compare them to actual results or situations and follow up on differences. Typically, cross training helps to deter fraud, but in this case, it is unlikely cross training would have been effective due to the highly technical aspects of IT operations.

2. As part of the vendor set up process, the accounting clerk could make a simple online inquiry using the vendor's name to determine if they exist or supply the types of goods and services appropriate to the entity or function, or both. Additionally, purchasing frequency reports might indicate purchasing patterns, which are outside the norm or are not consistent with management's expectations.

3. Originating department management should thoroughly review all vendors and purchases for propriety and reasonableness. When short-staffed or during peak service periods this is not always possible. Periodic training to remind operational personnel of the importance of internal controls, among other things, should be considered.

4. Using technology, vendor names and addresses can be matched against employee names and addresses as well as other external reliable databases. In detailed substantive tests or tests of controls, the auditor can determine if the purchase appears reasonable in light of the entity and the originating or benefiting function or department. Analytical procedures would also likely be an effective tool in detecting this situation.

5. Using either internal accounting staff or external auditors, the city manager should begin an investigation to determine whether fraud has occurred and to what extent. The investigation should cover at least the department in question and should probably be extended to other selected areas as well. The city manager should, at a minimum, document the situation and what was done to date. The city manager should also consult legal counsel to determine if the state Department of Law Enforcement should be notified and if so at what point. Additionally, the city manager should discuss the situation with the council members and the external auditor. Other responses to this question will vary based on the experience and attitudes of participants.

Knowledge check solutions

1.

    a. Incorrect. Riverside is located in a major metropolitan area.

    b. Incorrect. Population has been decreasing the last 20 years in Riverside.

    c. Incorrect. The majority of the residents of Riverside work in other areas of the metropolitan area.

    d. Correct. Riverside does employ about one half the number of people it did 20 years ago.

2.

    a. Incorrect. The IT manager position was created four years ago when the city installed its current financial management system.

    b. Incorrect. Because of the below market salary offered, very few individuals applied for the IT manager position when it was first advertised.

    c. Correct. The IT manager gradated from a small out of state college.

    d. Incorrect. The IT manager position is responsible for overseeing operation of the financial management system and for administering the city's internal and external network, website, and social media.

Chapter 3

Suggested solutions to Case 3

1. This case represents a potential fraud risk resulting from management override. In this case, management at the very top "bends the rules," which sets the tone for the entire organization. Additionally, the existence of a discretionary fund accessible only to the president of the university was used for various expenses some of which were excessive or unnecessary.

2. In this case, the state legislature has placed pressure on the college's board of trustees to achieve statutory educational and research benchmarks. This pressure appears to have caused the board to rush the process of selecting a new college president. It appears from the case information, some established recruiting and hiring policies may have been omitted or circumvented due to this pressure.

3. Because this case deals with management override, it would be difficult to implement effective controls as all persons in the university ultimately report to the president. However, the university might have found an anonymous fraud hotline effective in this case because the staff was not successful in executing controls effectively due to the involvement of the president. In addition, the university could have implemented controls over the president's discretionary account at the Board of Trustees level. To eliminate/reduce the pressure put on

the personnel director during the hiring process, the university could establish an independent search committee which would report to the entire board. In addition, the university could implement policies prohibiting board members from directing the work of staff other than the president (or acting president).

4. A review of any minutes kept by the President Selection Committee might reveal selection committee members were willing to circumvent established recruiting and hiring procedures. Reviewing minutes of college boards and committees might have indicated the pressure put on members to make decisions in the president's interest. Preliminary inquiries of college management and staff might also detect this situation. During these inquiries the auditor might also ask about the existence of any discretionary funds. Substantive tests of details or compliance tests related to controls over recruiting, hiring, purchasing and cash disbursements (assuming there are properly designed controls in place) might detect this situation. Utilizing technology, the auditor could generate a report of disbursements from the president's discretionary account (if the auditor was aware of its existence).

Knowledge check solutions

1.
    a. Correct. Upstate College is a small college in the northeast United States.
    b. Incorrect. Upstate College has had financial difficulties the last 10 years and is not in good financial condition.
    c. Incorrect. There are 15 members on the board of trustees.
    d. Incorrect. Due to the financial difficulties, the college has had difficulty attracting highly qualified faculty.

2.
    a. Incorrect. Nelson Odom is the chairman of the board of trustees.
    b. Incorrect. Upstate College does conduct FBI background checks.
    c. Correct. Tuan Nguyen is the personnel director.
    d. Incorrect. The board wishes the president to be in place by mid-May.

3.
    a. Incorrect. The new president is from a small college in Minnesota not Missouri.
    b. Incorrect. The chairman of the board refers to the new president as a real go-getter.
    c. Incorrect. The new president is from a small college in Minnesota not a large college.
    d. Correct. Cathryn Johnson is the new president.

Chapter 4

Suggested solutions to Case 4

1. Generally, the city's P-Card policies and procedures appear adequate, although they could have been expanded. In this case, the main problem was the issue of little or no oversight of the P-Card program. Periodic reviews of the various purchases, purchasers, and procedures might have discovered the fraud outlined in this case.

2. Because periodic oversight of the policies and procedures does not appear to have occurred or was ineffective, the city could have used technology to produce exception reports for purchase activity by vendor and purchases outside the normal purchasing cycle. Such reports might have noted unusual vendor activity such as on-line dating services, florist shops, and lingerie stores. In addition, reports might have noted patterns such a biweekly restaurant charges on the same night every month.

3. The amounts purchased and misappropriated were small in nature and consistent in volume. In some cases, they were also for items that could have been realistically used by the department.

4. Audit procedures to test procurement card controls and activity could include the following:

   - Review of policies and procedures for adequacy
   - Review of compensating controls and procedures for adequacy
   - Inquiries of personnel regarding potential fraudulent procurement card transactions
   - Compliance tests of controls either separately for procurement card transactions or for any procurement card disbursement selected in general cash disbursements/purchasing compliance tests
   - Substantive tests of details either separately for procurement card transactions or for any procurement card disbursement selected in general cash disbursements/purchasing tests
   - Review of vendor activity levels for selected vendors
   - Analysis of the number and total amount of transactions per card, department, vendor, and so forth and comparison to prior year

Knowledge check solutions

1.

    a. Incorrect. Accounts payable personnel review the P-Card statement for receipts that are attached.

    b. Correct. Employees sign the P-Card statement indicating they have reviewed the purchases and are authorizing them for payment.

    c. Incorrect. All employees being given P-Card privileges sign a P-Card authorization and agreement form.

    d. Incorrect. Each employee assigned a P-Card is responsible for reconciling his or her monthly statement and attaching the receipts.

2.

    a. Correct. An employee's immediate supervisor reviews the employee's P-Card statement and all related receipts.

    b. Incorrect. The supervisor follows up with the employee if any receipts are missing or if any charges appear questionable.

    c. Incorrect. An employee's immediate supervisor is required to review the employee's P-Card statement and all related receipts.

    d. Incorrect. Accounts payable personnel review the P-Card statement for the proper signatures (employee and supervisor).

3.

    a. Correct. The CFO reserves the right to review any P-Card statement activity at any time.

    b. Incorrect. An exception report is electronically transmitted each day to the CFO.

    c. Incorrect. All dollar and transaction limits, as well as allowable merchant codes, are programmed by the issuing financial institution into the card.

    d. Incorrect. The P-Card authorization and agreement form is signed by employees being given P-Card privileges, their immediate supervisors, and their department directors.

Chapter 5

Suggested solutions to Case 5

1. The cyber fraud in this case is a legitimate looking but fraudulent email that is sent to the city manager. This type of cyber fraud is spoofing.

2. Responses to this question will vary based on the experience and attitudes of the participants.

3. Responses to this question will vary based on the experience and attitudes of the participants.

Knowledge check solutions

1.

    a. Incorrect. Vishing is done with a cell phone, not phishing.

    b. Correct. Phishing involves email messages that appear to come from legitimate business or government sources.

    c. Incorrect. A rod and reel are used for fishing, not phishing. Email is usually used for phishing.

    d. Incorrect. A botnet is used for a denial of service attack, not for phishing.

2.

    a. Incorrect. A rootkit attacks the operating system, not an application system.

    b. Incorrect. A backdoor allows unauthorized access to the system, not a specific application program.

    c. Incorrect. A Trojan horse is a stand-alone program and does not attack a specific application.

    d. Correct. A virus is a segment of computer code that attaches itself to a program, such as Microsoft Office, that is already loaded on the computer.

The AICPA publishes *CPA Letter Daily*, a free e-newsletter published each weekday. The newsletter, which covers the 10-12 most important stories in business, finance, and accounting, as well as AICPA information, was created to deliver news to CPAs and others who work with the accounting profession. Besides summarizing media articles, commentaries, and research results, the e-newsletter links to television broadcasts and videos and features reader polls. *CPA Letter Daily*'s editors scan hundreds of publications and websites, selecting the most relevant and important news so you don't have to. The newsletter arrives in your inbox early in the morning. To sign up, visit smartbrief.com/CPA.

Do you need high-quality technical assistance? The AICPA Auditing and Accounting Technical Hotline provides non-authoritative guidance on accounting, auditing, attestation, and compilation and review standards. The hotline can be reached at 877.242.7212.

Learn More

Continuing Professional Education

Thank you for selecting the American Institute of Certified Public Accountants as your continuing professional education provider. We have a diverse offering of CPE courses to help you expand your skillset and develop your competencies. Choose from hundreds of different titles spanning the major subject matter areas relevant to CPAs and CGMAs, including:

- Governmental and not-for-profit accounting, auditing, and updates
- Internal control and fraud
- Audits of employee benefit plans and 401(k) plans
- Individual and corporate tax updates
- A vast array of courses in other areas of accounting and auditing, controllership, management, consulting, taxation, and more!

Get your CPE when and where you want

- Self-study training options that includes on-demand, webcasts, and text formats with superior quality and a broad portfolio of topics, including bundled products like –
  - ➤ CPExpress® online learning for immediate access to hundreds of one- to four-credit hour online courses for just-in-time learning at a price that is right
  - ➤ Annual Webcast Pass offering live Q&A with experts and unlimited access to the scheduled lineup, all at an incredible discount.
- Staff training programs for audit, tax and preparation, compilation, and review
- Certificate programs offering comprehensive curriculums developed by practicing experts to build fundamental core competencies in specialized topics
- National conferences presented by recognized experts
- Affordable courses on-site at your organization – visit **aicpalearning.org/on-site** for more information.
- Seminars sponsored by your state society and led by top instructors. For a complete list, visit **aicpalearning.org/publicseminar**.

Take control of your career development

The AICPA's Competency and Learning website at **https://competency.aicpa.org** brings together a variety of learning resources and a self-assessment tool, enabling tracking and reporting of progress toward learning goals.

Visit www.AICPAStore.com to browse our CPE selections.

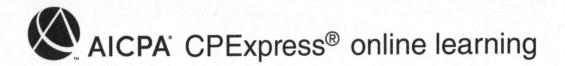

AICPA

Your strategic learning partner

Let us help prepare your staff for the future.

What is your current approach to learning? One size does not fit all. Your organization is unique, and your approach to learning and competency should be, too. But where do you start? Choose a strategic partner to help you assess competencies and gaps, design a customized learning plan, and measure and maximize the ROI of your learning and development initiatives.

We offer a wide variety of learning programs for finance professionals at every stage of their career.

AICPA Learning resources can help you:
- Create a learning culture to attract and retain talent
- Enrich staff competency and stay current on changing regulations
- Sharpen your competitive edge
- Capitalize on emerging opportunities
- Meet your goals and positively impact your bottom line
- Address CPE/CPD compliance

Flexible learning options include:
- On-site training
- Conferences
- Webcasts
- Certificate programs
- Online self-study
- Publications

An investment in learning can directly impact your bottom line. Contact an AICPA learning consultant to begin your professional development planning.

Call: 800.634.6780, option 1
Email: AICPALearning@aicpa.org